FORD
CONSUL/ZEPHYR/ZODIAC MK2

Michael Allen

CONTENTS

Foulis

Haynes

A FOULIS Motoring Book

First published 1987

© **Haynes Publishing Group**

Published by:
Haynes Publishing Group,
Sparkford, Near Yeovil,
Somerset BA22 7JJ

Haynes Publications Inc.
861 Lawrence Drive, Newbury
Park, California 91320, USA

British Library Cataloguing in Publication Data
Allen, Michael, *1939 Mar. 11–*
 Ford Consul/Zephyr/Zodiac Mk. II super profile.—(Super profile)
 1. Consul automobile—History
 2. Zephyr automobile—History
 3. Zodiac automobile—History
 I. Title   II. Series
 629.2'222   TL215.F7
 ISBN 0-85429-531-3

Editor: Robert Iles
Series photographer: Andrew Morland
Road tests: Courtesy of *Autocar* and *Motor*
Page layout: Peter Kay
Printed in England, by:
J.H. Haynes & Co. Ltd

Titles in the *Super Profile* series

Ariel Square Four (F388)
BMW R69 & R69S (F387)
Brough Superior SS100 (F365)
BSA A7 & A10 (F446)
BSA Bantam (F333)
BSA Gold Star (F483)
BSA M20 & M21 (F485)
Honda CB750 sohc (F351)
International Norton (F365)
KSS Velocette (F444)
Matchless G3L & G80 (F455)
MV Agusta America (F334)
Norton Commando (F335)
Norton International (F365)
Norton Manx (F452)
Sunbeam S7 & S8 (F363)
Triumph Thunderbird (F353)
Triumph Trident (F352)
Triumph Bonneville (F453)
Velocette KSS (F444)
Vincent Twins (F460)

AC/Ford/Shelby Cobra (F381)
Austin A30/A35 (F469)
Austin-Healey 'Frogeye' Sprite (F343)
Austin-Healey 100/4 (F487)
Chevrolet Corvette (F432)
Datsun 240Z, 260Z and 280Z (F488)
Ferrari 250 GTO (F308)
Ferrari Daytona (F535)
Ferrari Dino (F576)
Fiat X1/9 (F341)
Ford 100E Anglia, Prefect & Popular (F470)
Ford Consul/Zephyr/Zodiac Mk 1 (F497)

Ford Cortina 1600E (F310)
Ford GT40 (F332)
Ginetta G15 (F496)
Jaguar E-Type (F370)
Jaguar D-Type & XKSS (F371)
Jaguar Mk 2 Saloons (F307)
Jaguar SS90 & SS100 (F372)
Jaguar XK120 & 140 (F573)
Lamborghini Countach (F553)
Lancia Stratos (F340)
Lotus Elan (F330)
Lotus Seven (F385)
MGB (F305)
MG Midget & Austin-Healey Sprite (except 'Frogeye') (F344)
Mini Cooper (F445)
Morris Minor Series MM (F412)
Morris Minor & 1000 (ohv) (F331)
Porsche 911 Carrera (F311)
Porsche 917 (F495)
Range Rover (F534)
Rolls-Royce Corniche (F411)
Triumph Stag (F342)
Triumph TR2/3/3A (F559)

Deltics (F430)
Great Western Kings (F426)
Gresley Pacifics (F429)
Intercity 125 (F428)
Royal Scots (F431)
V2 'Green Arrow' Class (F427)

Further titles in this series will be published at regular intervals. For information on new titles please contact your bookseller or write to the publisher.

153 B55 has engine no.
298958.

153 B55 has engine no.
298958.

FOREWORD

In February 1956, anyone looking closely at the new Mk2 Consul Zephyr Zodiac range, studying the specifications, and taking into account the pedigree, would quickly conclude that here was a new car which simply could not fail to succeed.

There had been "Mk2" versions of established cars before, and have been many since, sometimes showing improvements over the preceding model but quite often not doing so in overall terms, whilst, occasionally actually proving to be inferior to what had gone before – change for change's sake having tarnished some once-proud model names.

The original Consul/Zephyr range had been a remarkable success, winning not only massive sales, but international rallies too, plus the acclaim of such notable motoring personalities of the day as Raymond Mays, Laurence Pomeroy Jun., and John Bolster. Now, here was a Mk2 version offering measurably more of the very qualities which had guaranteed the original car's success, and all packaged in a more commodius bodyshell with such well-balanced proportions that many would buy these cars on the basis of their good looks alone.

Thirty years later, the big Mk2

Fords are in demand once again by many of the enthusiasts who form today's thriving classic-car movement. Some, valuing both the model's common-sense straightforward mechanical simplicity and handsome appearance in these days of expensive to maintain "high-tech" cars with their low-drag factor anonymity, run their Mk2s on an everyday basis with great success, whilst others keep a "mint" example as a treasured second-car to be exhibited proudly at some of the many summer shows and parades now catering for the old-car owner. Several of these enthusiasts are amongst those who willingly gave assistance in the preparation of this book, by loaning rare photographs, literature etc., or locating, and providing cars for the purpose of many of the illustrations, and my thanks in this respect go to: Dave Cropper, Howard Foottit, Dave Woodfield, Richard Pybus, Stuart Clarke, Eric Pearson, Philip Holliday, John Mather, Rae Whittles, Dave Goodwin, Ian Carey, Steve Newman, Nigel Humberstone, Nigel Palethorpe, John Walker, Chris Greensmith, Dave Barry, Dick Barry, the West Yorkshire Metropolitan Police, and photographer Andrew Morland. Thanks, too, to Steve Clark and Sheila Knapman of Ford

Photographic Services, and Anne Hall and Jeff Uren for the competition-Zephyr pictures. For permission to reproduce the engine/chassis number lists I'm most grateful to David Burgess-Wise of Ford Motor Company Public Affairs, and to Matthew Carter, of "Autocar", and John Thorpe, of "Motor", I am also very grateful for their permission to reproduce contemporary road test reports which featured in their respective magazines. Finally, my thanks to Stephen Pickles, and Stuart Clarke once again, for their contribution in the form of "Owners' Views".

Michael G. D. Allen

HISTORY

Family tree

Although the Ford Motor Co. (England) Ltd. had assembled the Model T at its Manchester factory since 1911, it was not until the 1930s, after occupying its new purpose-built plant at Dagenham and introducing the 8hp Y Type Ford, that the company established itself as one of the "big three" motor manufacturers in Britain. The model Y was an immediate success, and was quickly joined by the 10hp Model C which introduced the famous 1,172cc engine that was destined to power small-Fords for more than 25 years. Redesigned 8 and 10hp models appeared in the late 1930s, and these quickly evolved into the first of the long-running series of Anglia and Prefect models. The small cars had been joined by large, V8 engined models in 1935, these being available with either a 22hp or 30hp (3.6 litre) sidevalve engine, and bearing a marked similarity overall to the transatlantic Fords produced at that time by the parent company in Detroit.

Common features throughout the entire range were a six-volt electrical system, a sidevalve layout for the engines, a mechanically operated clutch, a three-speed gearbox with synchromesh between the upper two ratios, and torque tube drive to a spiral-bevel rear axle. The all drum braking systems were also mechanically operated, and the suspension arrangements consisted of a single transverse leaf spring at either end, with hydraulic shock absorbers. Separate chassis frames were employed, to which was fitted bodywork of steel construction with a fabric-covered roof centre section.

In 1945, following the cessation of hostilities in Europe, the Anglia and Prefect soon reappeared, with minor improvements incorporated into their specification but nevertheless being, in overall terms, virtually the same as their pre-war counterparts. Post war steel shortages resulted in Dagenham using their quota at first to just produce the small-car range, a policy which was also valid in view of the wartime petrol rationing which was not to be lifted for some considerable time. So it was not until late in 1947 that a post war V8 model was announced, and even then it was stated by Ford Chairman Sir Rowland Smith that production was to be strictly limited. To be known as the Pilot, the new car was based closely on the pre-war V8 Model 62, but with substantially restyled front and rear bodywork, and a much more comprehensive level of standard equipment. As announced, the Pilot was to have been powered by a narrow-bored version of the V8 engine rated at just 21hp, but the abandonment of the horsepower tax about this time resulted in the production models appearing with the larger-bored 30hp rated unit of 3.6 litres.

With the Pilot, Dagenham now had a high-quality, high-performance, prestige model, but its 30cwt bulk represented a lot of the then very scarce raw material as well as resulting in a high thirst for fuel which was another scarce commodity at that time. Also, there was a considerable gap in the Ford range between it and the 10hp Prefect, and it was with all of these thoughts in mind that the Dagenham design and engineering team began work in 1948 on a completely new range which, whilst taking over at the top from the Pilot, would also fill that important gap. These new cars, the Consul and the Zephyr Six, would be unveiled at Earls Court in October 1950.

With the full approval of the parent company, Dagenham discarded much previous Ford thinking during the development of this new range, with the result that a completely new bodyshell of monocoque construction was employed, the front end structure of which was designed to accommodate, for the first time anywhere, the revolutionary MacPherson strut independent front suspension system designed by the American Ford engineer of that name. This system feeds the suspension loads directly into the front scuttle structure, so eliminating the need for a separate subframe on which to mount the then conventional wishbone type independent front suspension installation in a monocoque bodyshell. Thus, Dagenham were able to produce a bodyshell offering similar internal accommodation to that of the V8 Pilot, but within rather more compact external dimensions and at a useful weight saving over the previous separate body and chassis construction. The new engines too, a $1\frac{1}{2}$ litre four-cylinder and a $2\frac{1}{4}$ litre "six", also broke new ground for Ford in that overhead valves were employed. More importantly, however, was that these new units were the first to go into production featuring a bore diameter which was somewhat wider than the piston stroke. The designers, in fact had taken full advantage of the abandonment of the horsepower tax which had previously resulted in narrow-bored engines due to the power being calculated for taxation purposes on the bore size only.

The adoption of a hydraulically operated clutch, an open propellor shaft, and a hypoid bevel final drive assembly in a rear axle located by longitudinally mounted semi-elliptic leaf springs, were other departures from past Dagenham practice, as was also the new all hydraulic braking system. But the three-speed gearbox, and vacuum operated windscreen wipers were time-honoured Ford features which in fact would remain for many years yet.

At one stroke, Dagenham had not only jumped into the forefront of the inexpensive high-performance six-cylinder market, with the new Zephyr in fact having all the performance of the preceding V8 Pilot allied to a 25% improvement in fuel economy and a 20% reduction in purchase price, but also into the very important market for roomy bodied four-cylinder family cars which the company had not contested before. The new range met with considerable success, and was expanded in 1953 first with the addition of two-door convertible models, and then in October with the announcement of the luxuriously equipped Zephyr Zodiac saloon which was in effect a super de luxe edition of the standard Zephyr Six.

The Mk2 Range: Concept and Design

Also in 1953, the Consul/Zephyr range had been joined by the completely new Anglia and Prefect 100E models and a "new" Ford Popular, the latter actually being a detrimmed version of the preceding "upright" Anglia model. With this range established, and demand continually rising, there was no need at all to consider face-lifts for the Consul and Zephyr models with which it was proving impossible to meet the demand, and so attention at Dagenham was now turned to the development of an eventual replacement range.

Few criticisms had been levelled at the Mk1 Consul/Zephyr range as such, with teething troubles, too, being almost entirely absent, and so after three years of continuous production the model was very substantially the same as on its introduction. In fact, considerable praise had been directed at this model from many sources, and it was quite obvious at Dagenham that a restyled replacement must nevertheless be seen to be a genuine descendant of this very popular range. Although able to seat six people in reasonable comfort, the relatively compact Mk1 was not at its best in a six seater role, and it was in this respect where the most obvious room for improvement lay.

Considerable experience of monocoque construction had now been gained at Dagenham, as the new 100E range also featured an integrally constructed bodyshell, and in the light of this experience it was now possible to produce a usefully larger bodyshell with only a modest increase in weight. A 5in. increase in overall width was necessary to achieve the generous six-seater capacity required, and this was accompanied by an appropriate increase in length which, in addition to providing more kneeroom, front seat adjustment, and luggage space at the rear, also maintained the correct visual proportions. A wider track and longer wheelbase, with the consequential improvement in riding and ultimate handling qualities, was a useful natural outcome of this overall enlargement. The general layout was unchanged, with the engine bay once again differing slightly in length between the four- and six-cylinder models. A counterbalanced bonnet top was a welcome improvement. The front wings were bolted on, but at the rear a constructional change was evident with the wings now being included in the integral construction, whereas previously these too, had been bolt on panels. Much slimmer pillars and a virtually uninterrupted all-round glass area was a notable feature, with the very large expanse of glass offsetting somewhat the relative weight savings made in the all-steel structure by comparison with the previous model. Actually improving upon the excellent torsional rigidity of the earlier cars, now, was a steel inner membrane running the full length of the lower outboard box sections formed by the welded-up inner and outer sills. No fundamental changes were necessary in respect of the running gear, and the independent front suspension consisted once again of the MacPherson struts located at the top in the inner wing from where they transmitted the suspension loads into the sturdy scuttle/bulkhead structure, whilst at the bottom, being located by the track control arms and the forward mounted transverse anti-roll bar. Controlling the direction of the front wheels via a three piece track rod arrangement was a worm and peg type steering box with a slightly lower ratio than previously, thus requiring a similar steering effort to that of the lighter Mk1 cars. The wider track, and a much roomier front wheel arch allowed a usefully improved steering lock, so removing one of the two legitimate criticisms aimed at the previous model, whilst wider front brake drums, allowing an appreciably greater brake lining area, removed the other. Long semi elliptic leaf springs again located the back axle, and the same wheel and tyre sizes were retained, although the rims were new with a slightly different offset.

In Mk1 form, the short stroke engines had proved capable of withstanding considerable power increases when fitted with any of the wide variety of performance equipment which became available for these units from outside sources. However, as the original bore centres had been very widely spaced with a view to possible enlargement without losing the very desirable water jacketing which encircled each individual cylinder, greater cylinder capacities, rather than very high compression ratios or multiple carburettors, were chosen as the basis for an increase in power output. A very slightly longer-throw crankshaft was also used to give a further increase in capacity whilst retaining the oversquare dimensions, with an enlargement of the bearing journal diameters now to maintain a substantial overlap as before despite the longer throw. These changes resulted in capacities now of 1.7 litres and 2.55 litres for the four- and six-cylinder units, respectively, from which a useful power increase was provided without the need for other power-boosting modifications. Apart from the moving-round of the fuel pump operating lobe on the camshaft (to miss the longer crank throw), the overhead valve gear was standard Mk1 throughout. There was only a modest increase in compression ratio – to 7.8:1 – and single Zenith carburettors were again employed. A larger diameter clutch was a new feature on the six-cylinder Zephyrs and Zodiacs only, whilst the internals of the three-speed gearbox remained almost wholly the Mk1 items. Raised axle ratios however, for both the four- and six-cylinder cars, promised usefully quicker maximum and cruising speeds in top gear, whilst the higher speeds now available in second gear

would improve the overtaking abilities considerably in the important 30 to 50mph bracket. The continued lack of synchromesh with which to assist the engagement of first gear was something of a disappointment, particularly so as the higher gearing would make the selection of this ratio whilst in motion a more frequent occurrence now. The vacuum operated windscreen wipers were another link with Ford's past that would lead to some, although by no means universal, disapproval.

Despite the fact that the new models were based closely on what were now very well-proven mechanical elements, and that much existing tooling was to be utilised, extensive prototype testing took place on an almost world-wide scale throughout much of 1955. At the beginning of the year, prototypes which apart from being devoid of tell-tale badges and scripts, were otherwise almost identical visually to the eventual production cars, were on test in northern Europe, and by the end of the year the production specification was finalised.

Production

Dagenham were now in an enviable position, with a new model ready to go into production at a time when, even after five years, the sales of the existing model were still rising steadily; although production of the Mk1 now was coming close to meeting the demand. The Mk2 entered production quietly in January 1956, with a short

build-up period prior to the launch on February 21st when "The Three Graces", as the new cars were billed, received immediate acclaim on the basis of their styling alone. This new appearance was, as perhaps was to be expected, a rather discreet representation of the parent company's current products from across the Atlantic, whose shapes lended themselves surprisingly well to European dimensions.

Once again, the four-cylinder Consul was seen to display deliberate economies in respect of trim and equipment. A moulded rubber floorcovering, a single horn, and the availability of such as the armrest/doorpulls, and bumper overriders only as extra-cost options, all indicating that this was the economy model in the range, aimed at providing good performance and durability in a comfortable overall package at the lowest practicable first cost. Additional luxuries such as the carpeting and armrests etc. were to be found as standard equipment on the Zephyr, whilst the Zodiac was once again the very fully equipped top-of-the-range car, identified as before by dual tone paintwork, whitewall tyres and, unlike the previous model, now with its own distinctive grille.

Two-door convertible versions of the Consul and Zephyr were immediately available, and in October 1956 were joined by a similar variation of the Zodiac. Estate cars based on all three models also arrived in the October, having been developed by coachbuilders E.D. Abbott on similar lines to the conversions they had first offered on the Mk1 Fords late in 1954. In addition to the overdrive option already on the six-cylinder cars, now was the availability of fully automatic transmission, thus widening the appeal further of what was now an extremely comprehensive range being offered at price levels in keeping with past Ford practice.

Despite the effects of a dispute outside the company which nevertheless affected Ford production, and then the Suez crisis and its attendant fuel difficulties, the Mk2s sold well from the start, and in 1957 production reached the peak rate achieved two years earlier by the Mk1 cars. More than half of this production was destined for overseas, with built-up cars being shipped across the Atlantic and elsewhere whilst knocked-down cars were heading for Ford assembly plants as near as Belgium, and as far away as Australia and New Zealand. For 1958, a Consul De Luxe, offering broadly similar trim and equipment to that of the Zodiac was a welcome addition to the range which would satisfy those wishing for four-cylinder economy, but rather more luxury than the basic Consul. All three cars also now acquired new recirculating ball steering gear and a redesigned column gear change linkage. A 15% increase in sales for that year was nevertheless followed by slight styling changes aimed at further increasing the appeal, and early in 1959 the "Low Line" models appeared. Characterized by their flatter roof panel, the Low-Line cars featured additional bright-metal trim externally and completely redesigned interior appointments, the latter putting some emphasis on increased passenger safety with the provision now of crushable sunvisors and a padded facia top. No price rise accompanied these changes, and the range continued unaltered until late in 1960 when front wheel disc brakes became available as an extra-cost option. The popularity of these resulted in them being absorbed into the standard specification (with an appropriate price adjustment) during 1961. Sealed-beam headlamps were introduced at the same time, and it was with this specification that the Mk2 range was discontinued in April 1962.

Reasons for Discontinuation

As a result of an expansion programme begun in 1954, considerably greater production capacity would allow Ford of Britain to offer an appreciably wider range of products during the 1960s than had previously been possible. This enabled the company to plan a new big-car range which could be aimed rather more up market than the Mk2 models, particularly so in respect of the Zodiac which was to become even more of a separate model in its own right. New medium sized models were to appear, to sell between an all new small car, the 105E Anglia, and this new up market big-car range. The 105E Anglia was in fact the first of the planned 1960s models to appear, late in 1959, and was followed by the 1340cc engined Classic in 1961, the full title of which was Consul Classic 315. This was the first indication that the Consul name would eventually disappear from the big-car range, and resulted in the last of the Mk2 Consuls having a "375" suffix added to their name, and even being badged accordingly, whilst production overlapped with the Consul Classic 315. This situation continued until the Mk2 range was deleted in April 1962 upon the introduction of the big Mk3 models of which the four-cylinder car was to be known as the Zephyr 4.

Motorsport

By the time the Mk2 range appeared, a Ford competition department had been established for more than three years, during which time several class wins, and outright victory in the Monte Carlo Rally had been achieved by "works" Mk1 Zephyrs. Additionally, a privately entered Zephyr had won the East African Safari in 1955, thus making the Mk1 Zephyr a "hard act to follow", as the saying goes, in respect of competition work.

Nevertheless, despite its increase in size alone giving an impression that it would perhaps be rather less handy as a competition car, overall, the Mk2 Zephyr was destined to build quite considerably on the achievements of the previous model, with great success coming right away in the 1956 Alpine Rally. Three of the new cars were entered for this event, all running in the modified category and so equipped with raised compression ratio cylinder heads and a triple Zenith carburettor layout. Unfortunately, a faulty ignition coil caused Anne Hall's Zephyr to lose time, but T.C. "Cuth" Harrison, and Denis Scott drove their Zephyrs to first and second places in the up-to-2600cc class, this feat earning each of them one of the rare Alpine Cups which were awarded to any car completing the road sections (which included numerous Alpine passes) without penalty, with the final results then being decided on a penalty system applicable to the "special stages" only.

The Suez crisis caused the cancellation of many events soon after this, although the Dutch RAC West did manage to stage their International Tulip Rally in the spring of 1957, in which the Zephyrs won both the Team Prize (which was normally awarded to the three least penalized cars of the same model), and the Ladies Cup (Anne Hall). Much more action was seen in 1958, starting with the Monte Carlo Rally in which four Mk2s were amongst the 59 cars (out of 303 starters) who made it to the finish. The best placed Mk2 was the privately entered Zodiac of R. Nelleman who won the over-2000cc class, whilst Edward Harrison's works-entered Zephyr was the only one of the 85 Paris starters to survive the blizzard conditions in the Jura mountains and the Massif Central to get through to Monte Carlo. A class win quickly followed in the RAC Rally in March, when Denis Scott and Ken Armstrong brought their triple SU carburettor equipped Zephyr in to win the over-2000cc GT category, with an Aston Martin and a 3.4 Jaguar, no less, taking second and third places respectively, behind the Zephyr. Another Alpine Cup was won in July, when Edward Harrison drove a standard Zephyr to a class win in what proved to be a particularly tough Alpine in which more than half the 58 strong entry failed to finish.

Meanwhile, what should have been a much-publicised outright win, Team Prize, and Ladies Cup, by privately entered Zephyrs in the 1958 East African Safari, was marred by some odd decisions at the finish when all the best-placed Fords, including the class winning 100E Anglia, were handed additional penalties for alleged technical offences. These allegations were in fact groundless, but by the time the situation was sorted out much of the impact had been lost. The following year saw the first works-entered Zephyrs in this event, and although they failed to repeat the success of the Kopperud brothers who had beaten Mercedes into second place the previous year, Denis Scott and Edward Harrison finished second and third respectively behind one of the surviving German cars, and combined with the locally entered Zodiac of Young and Baillon to take the Team Prize. Success quickly followed in the Tulip Rally, with Peter Riley taking third place overall and winning the 1600cc-2600cc class from

Shock's Mercedes 220. Cuth Harrison and Gerry Burgess also finished strongly in their Zephyrs, and in combination with Riley's car gained another Team Prize for the Mk2 Ford. First, second, and third, by Peter Riley, Cuth Harrison, and Edward Harrison in the over-2000cc GT Saloon category in the Alpine Rally in July resulted in three more Alpine Cups and yet another Team Prize.

Meanwhile, on the racing circuits, too, the Zephyr was enjoying success. In 1958, in his privately entered Zephyr, Jeff Uren had finished runner up in the first BRSCC Saloon Car Championships, being beaten by Jack Sears' works-prepared Austin Westminster. For the 1959 series however, Jeff Uren was receiving works support, and this resulted in the preparation of a particularly potent Zephyr which produced 168bhp from its Raymond Mays modified engine. Girling disc brakes had already been seen on some of the rally Zephyrs, and these were now included in the racing Zephyr specification, along with slightly lowered, and considerably stiffened suspension. An outright win in the BRSCC Championship was now added to the 1959 successes, with Jeff Uren clinching the title at Brands Hatch in August. Finally, in November, Gerry Burgess finished off an excellent year for the Zephyr with outright victory in the RAC Rally.

A class win (over-2000cc GT category) by private entrants D. Handley and D. Harvey in their modified Zodiac in the 1960 "Monte", was followed by the Team Prize going to the "works" Zephyrs in the Safari at Easter time; but, a new penalty/handicap system on the Alpine Rally that year proved to be just too severe, and no more Alpine Cups were collected on the event despite the Zephyrs being equipped with 150bhp Mays-tuned engines. More emphasis was now being placed on the new 105E Anglia

for competition work, but a full Zephyr team were alongside these in Kenya for the 1961 Safari from which the Zephyrs emerged once again as the Team Prize winners, with Anne Hall's third place overall and Ladies Cup on her first Safari being a notable achievement indeed.

Success Review

There are several respects in which a car can achieve success, usually depending considerably on what its prime purpose is, and any passenger car which sells well amongst its contemporaries can rightly claim success.

As a passenger, or family car, the big Mk2 Fords offered more accommodation for the family than could be purchased elsewhere at the price, and this, coupled with an overall economy of operation usually associated with smaller cars, no doubt contributed largely to the fact that over 650,000 Mk2s were sold during their six-year production run. This figure alone, which is higher than that of any other British model throughout the same period, and of which approximately half represented export sales, is quite sufficient to claim that this was indeed a very successful model. In motorsport too, as we have seen, there was also success, with the Zephyr winning the BRSCC Saloon Car Championship. In addition to which there were the successes achieved in international rallying in which the Zephyrs proved capable of taking class and other awards in every type of event staged in Britain and across Europe, whilst in Africa sharing with the Mercedes 220 complete domination of the East African Safari from 1958 to 1961. In fact, the records appear to show that with its wins, class wins, Alpine Cups, Team Prizes, Ladies Cups etc., this model gained more international rallying awards than any other car during the same period. This is all the more remarkable when it is realised that if this big, comfortable family saloon was fitted with engine modifications such as triple SU carburettors, it was then often forced by the regulations to compete directly with large engined two-seaters and other expensive high-powered Gran Turismo machinery, and under conditions in which these types were supposed to excel. There have certainly been other British cars to achieve similar successes in their day. Success in these two spheres, however, does not always bring the right rewards. One of Britain's most famous postwar cars, the BMC Mini, achieved very high volume sales in the 1960s, whilst also carving out for itself an illustrious competition career, and on these two counts alone has rightly been judged an extremely successful car, although, sadly, it consistantly lost money for its manufacturer.

In contrast, despite being sold at prices which other British manufacturers simply could not meet for this type and quality of car, the Mk2 range always made healthy profits for the Ford Motor Company. The top selling British model of its time, an award winning rally car and championship winning racing saloon, and a money-spinner too – the big Mk2 Fords were indeed a success.

EVOLUTION

Evolution

The chassis and engine numbers were the same when the cars were new. This number is prefixed by the model identification code, and appears on the chassis plate fixed on the right-hand-side of the engine compartment front panel and is, in addition, stamped into the front suspension upper mounting point on the right-hand-side of the car. The engine number is stamped into the horizontal surface on the cylinder block adjacent to the right-hand-side engine mounting bracket.

Model identification, January 1956 to October 1961.

204E = 4 cyl',
205E = 4 cyl' left-hand-drive,
206E = 6 cyl',
207E = 6 cyl' left-hand-drive

Model identification, November/December 1961.

Consul: 41A = saloon, 42A = De Luxe, 43A = convertible,
44A = estate car
Zephyr: 51A = saloon, 52A = convertible, 53A = estate car
Zodiac: 61A = saloon, 62A = convertible, 63A = estate car

On cars produced from January 1962 onwards the letter A is replaced by the letter B.

January 26th 1956: First production Zephyrs and Zodiacs assembled.
February 1956 (early): First production Consuls assembled.
February 21st 1956: The Mk2 range announced as "The Three Graces", with the range comprising the Consul (£781), Consul convertible (£946), Zephyr (£872), Zephyr convertible (£1,111), and Zodiac (£969). A heater/demister was an extra-cost option on the Consul and Zephyr, with a radio optional on all three models. A power-operated top (standard on the Zephyr convertible) was optional on the Consul at £75. In addition to its external embellishments, standard equipment on the Zodiac only was leather upholstery, electric clock, cigar lighter, vanity mirror, and windscreen washers. A Borg-Warner overdrive was optional equipment on the six-cylinder cars only at £63.
May 1956: Redesigned exhaust system on Consul saloon, with the convertible retaining the original system.
August 1956: Rear axle half shafts with 24 splines, and appropriate new differential gears, replaced the original 16-spine shafts. (This modification was as a result of early Mk2 Zephyr police cars suffering from broken half shafts soon after entering service).
October 1956: Chrome trim introduced on rear screen pillars. Horizontal flutes on previously flat back panel on Consul and Zephyr. Zodiac convertible introduced at £1253, with all usual Zodiac amenities including interior sunvisors which were still omitted from the Consul/Zephyr convertibles. Estate car conversions available from E.D. Abbott as brand-new cars at £1028 (Consul), £1028 (Consul), £1118 (Zephyr), and £1223 for the Zodiac. Borg-Warner

automatic transmission announced as an optional extra at £187 on the six-cylinder saloons and estate cars only. Redesigned exhaust system introduced on six-cylinder models except convertibles.
February 1957: Factory price increase on all models, with saloon prices now £818 (Consul), £916 (Zephyr), and £1013 for the Zodiac.
October 1957: Consul De Luxe saloon announced at £871, featuring Zodiac style interior appointments, but without the heater which was still optional equipment. External De Luxe recognition features were a second colour applied to the roof, and chrome-plated rear lamp surrounds. Restyled grille introduced on the Zephyr, and incorporating Zodiac style side lamp units. Front seat centre arm rests introduced as standard on Zephyr and Zodiac in place of previous rear seat arm rests which were now deleted. Redesigned front seat frame on all three models, and foam rubber overlay in both front and rear seats. Redesigned rear screen chrome trim on all models. Recirculating ball steering box, and concentric gearchange mechanism introduced on all models.
May 1958: Single venturi carburettor replaced double venturi type on Consul only, from engine number 204E 120679.
July 1958: Cadmium-plated rear spring front hanger bolts introduced to reduce any tendency to "squeak", from engine numbers 204E 133837 and 206E 123995.
August 1958: Improved circlips in manual gearbox (not applicable to overdrive), from engine numbers 204E 135726 and 206E 126837. New pressed-steel water valve assembly replaced die-cast assembly in heater unit to eliminate possible seizure of valve.
September 1958: New connecting rods with wider "I" section fitted to engines from 204E 137798 and 206E 129301.

October 1958: Screw and locknut adjustment provided for convertible front seat backrest angle. Improved safety front door lock in which the interior handle is inoperative when the door-sill button is in the locked position.

November 1958: Improved handbrake cable with thicker inner cable to eliminate any tendency to buckle when handbrake is being released, from engine numbers 204E 153938 and 206E 142305.

February 1959: Low-Line models introduced. Flatter roof panel, new windscreen surround to take deeper screen, and new belt-rail section behind redesigned facia. Additional chrome-plated and rustless bright-metal embellishment, and redesigned interior appointments including safety padding and collapsible sunvisors. Original gearchange mechanism readopted, but now enclosed in new steering column shroud. Track rod assemblies of increased thread diameter with larger diameter and greater length adjusting sleeve introduced. All these changes from engine numbers 204E 170644 and 206E 154227.

March 1959: Further improvements to gearbox mainshaft bearing circlip.

April 1959: Purchase tax reduction to £773 (Consul), £865 (Zephyr), and £957 for the Zodiac.

December 1959: Deeper throat in gearbox extension housing to improve mainshaft bearing circlip retention, from approximate engine numbers 204E 230000 and 206E 220000.

July 1960: Stud and nut fixing of fuel pump to engine block changed to bolt fixing, from engine numbers 204E 271727 and 206E 264175.

September 1960: Front disc brakes available as optional equipment on all models at £29.15s.. Conversion kit for earlier cars available at £32 plus fitting charge. Paper element carburettor air cleaner on home market cars replacing the washable gauze type

(Zephyr) and oil bath (Zodiac). Oil bath retained on export models.

January 1961: Redesigned gearbox mainshaft with nut fixing for speedometer drive gear in place of previous circlip. (Not applicable to overdrive models).

May 1961: Disc brakes standardised, and sealed beam headlamps introduced. Name script deleted from rear wing sides. Consul renamed "Consul 375" with boot lid badge ammended accordingly, and "375" appearing on the grille badge on the Consul De Luxe. Prices increased to £823 and £873 (Consul & Consul De Luxe), £907 (Zephyr) and £1012 (Zodiac).

April 1962: Mk2 range deleted with the announcement of the Mk3 models. A late further price increase resulted in final prices of £844 (Consul), £888 (Consul De Luxe), £1012 (Consul convertible), £1085 (Consul estate car), £942 (Zephyr), £1110 (Zephyr convertible) £1182 (Zephyr estate car), £1037 (Zodiac), £1325 (Zodiac convertible), £1285 (Zodiac estate car).

Approximate chassis numbers from introduction to September 1958

	204E (4 cyl')	206E (6 cyl')
1956 Jan/February	0001	0001
October	26000	25750
1957 October	80500	75000
1958 September	145000	135000

Approximate mid-month engine numbers from October 1958 to

October 1961. Engine assembly was of course ahead of final vehicle assembly date, but as the chassis number corresponded to the engine installed when new, the following numbers give a guide to approximate car build date.

1958		
October	150894	140249
November	157323	144642
December	162555	148685
1959		
January	168779	153177
February	174760	158403
March	178693	162671
April	185143	168458
May	191435	175137
June	198020	180569
July	204806	186985
August	207510	190100
September	213861	197513
October	220080	204608
November	226624	211937
December	232700	219045
1960		
January	238853	225472
February	245727	232043
March	251251	239194
April	257133	247210
May	262002	253788
June	267679	260791
July	274540	267402
August	277639	270068
September	285285	274423
October	291438	278138
November	295821	281194
December	299615	285105
1961		
January	302923	287987
February	306744	291010
March	313189	294406
April	319977	298810
May	325637	303108
June	331301	307137
July	334512	310222
August	336433	311745
September	339654	315740
October	342271	317625

End of month chassis numbers of final numbering system with new prefix. These numbers did not follow consecutively from the earlier series.

1961		
November	A099662	A096585
December	A119917	A119599
1962		
January	B013804	B014012
February	B037589	B037810

Production ceased April 1962. Total engine production was greater than car production owing to the need for occasional replacement engines for cars in service, and small numbers for other applications. From 22nd December 1960 both the four- and six-cylinder units were added to the Ford engine exhange plan,

in which the customer's original engine was taken in against a new or fully reconditioned engine at an exchange price of £39 for the Consul and £53 for the Zephyr/Zodiac units. Exhange clutch assemblies were an

additional £5.15s and £6.0.6d for the four- and six-cylinder models, respectively.

SPECIFICATION

Specification

Type	Ford Consul Mk2 (4 cyl') Zephyr & Zodiac Mk2 (6 cyl')
Manufacturer's Type designation	204E (4 cyl') 206E (6 cyl')
Built	Dagenham, England. January 1956 – April 1962
Numbers made	Consul saloons and convertibles 350,244 Zephyr/Zodiac saloons and convertibles 301,417 (approximately 80,000 Zodiacs) Convertible production approximately 2% of the above totals Abbott estate cars (all models) 5,643 Australian station wagons (all models) 7,470 Australian pick-up/utilities (all models) 17,580 Dagenham pick-ups (all models) 46

Engine

Cylinder block	Cast iron, deep-skirt extending below crankshaft centre line. Four or six cylinders in-line, water jacketing encircling each individual cylinder.
Cylinder head	Cast iron, with wedge shaped combustion chambers and siamezed inlet ports. Valve guides machined directly in the cylinder head.
Valve gear	Overhead, operated by pushrods and rockers from side-mounted camshaft.
Crankshaft	Cast alloy steel, counterbalanced and with main and big-end journal overlap and hollow webs. Three main bearings (4 cyl'), and four main bearings on the six cylinder engine.
Capacity	1703cc (4 cyl') 2553cc (6 cyl')
Bore & stroke	82.55mm x 79.5mm
Compression ratio	7.8:1 (6.9:1 optional)
Maximum power (4 cyl')	59bhp (nett) @ 4,400rpm (55bhp with 6.9:1 CR)
Maximum power (6 cyl')	85 bhp (nett) @ 4,400rpm (81bhp with 6.9:1 CR)
Maximum torque (4 cyl')	91 lbf ft (nett) @ 2,300rpm (87 lbf ft with 6.9:1 CR)
Maximum torque (6 cyl')	133 lbf ft (nett) @ 2,000rpm (127 lbf ft with 6.9:1 CR)

Fuel system

Carburettor	Single Zenith downdraught incorporating an accelerator pump.
Fuel pump	AC mechanical, incorporating a vacuum pump for windscreen wiper operation.
Fuel tank capacity	$10^1/2$ gallons

Transmission

Clutch	Hydraulic. Single dry plate, 8 inch diameter (Consul) $8^1/2$ inch diameter (Zephyr/Zodiac).
Gearbox	3-speed constant mesh. Synchromesh on second and top gears.
Overdrive	Borg-Warner semi-automatic with freewheel operation at low speeds. 0.70 ratio. Optional equipment on 6-cylinder models only.
Automatic	Borg-Warner model DG 3-speed fully automatic gearbox and torque converter. Optional equipment on 6-cylinder models only.
Rear axle	Hypoid, three-quarter floating. 4.11:1 ratio (Consul), 3.9:1 ratio (Zephyr/Zodiac).

Overall gear ratios	Consul	Zephyr/Zodiac
first	11.67	11.08
second	6.75	6.4
top	4.11	3.9
Road speed/1,000rpm		
first	5.95mph	6.5mph
second	10.2	11.27
top	16.9	18.5
overdrive	–	26.4

6.70 x 13 tyres fitted to 6-cylinder estate cars and cars with automatic transmission raises overall gearing to approximately 19mph/1,000rpm.

Suspension

Front	Independent by MacPherson struts incorporating hydraulic telescopic shock absorbers. Coil springs.
Rear	Non independent. Longitudinally mounted semi-elliptic leaf springs of 6 leaves each (7 leaves for export and on estate cars). Lever arm hydraulic shock absorbers.

Steering

Worm and peg steering box mounted behind axle line. 16.8:1 ratio. Recirculating-ball steering box with 18.1:1 ratio from October 1957.

Turning circle — 34ft (Consul), 36ft (Zephyr/Zodiac).

Brakes

Girling hydraulic. 9 inch diameter drums on all four wheels with two leading shoes in the front drums, one leading and one trailing shoe in rear drums. 147 sq. inches total lining area. Later, $9^3/4$ inch diameter Girling disc brakes on front wheels, with vacuum servo assistance to all four wheels.

Wheels and tyres

Pressed steel disc wheels, five stud fixing. Rim diameter 13 inches, Rim width 4 inches, 5.90 x 13 tyres at 28 lbf/in² (Consul). Rim width $4^1/2$ inches 6.40 x 13 tyres at 24 lbf/in² tyres (Zephyr/Zodiac).

Electrical system

12 volt positive earth, 45 ampere hour battery (Consul), 57 ampere hour (Zephyr/Zodiac). Two brush generator and separate voltage control regulator.

Bodywork	4-door saloon, all steel welded integrally constructed body/chassis unit, with bolt-on front wings. Built by Briggs Motor Bodies, Dagenham.
	2-door convertible, built by Carbodies of Coventry on reinforced saloon floorpan.
	Estate cars converted by E.D. Abbott, Farnham, Surrey, from partially-built saloons.

Dimensions

Overall length, Consul	14ft 4in. prior to Feb' 1959. 14ft 6$\frac{1}{2}$in. Feb' 1959 onwards.
Overall length, Zephyr	14ft 10$\frac{1}{2}$in. prior to Feb' 1959. 14ft 11in. Feb' 1959 onwards.
Overall length, Zodiac	15ft 0$\frac{1}{2}$in.
Overall width, all models	5ft 9in.
Height, all models	5ft 2in. prior to Feb' 1959. 5ft 0$\frac{1}{2}$in. Feb' 1959 onwards.
Wheelbase, Consul	8ft 8$\frac{1}{2}$in.
Wheelbase, Zephyr/Zodiac	8ft 11in.
Track, all models	4ft 5in. front
	4ft 4in. rear

Weight (saloons)   22$\frac{1}{4}$cwt (Consul), 24cwt (Zephyr), 24$\frac{1}{2}$cwt (Zodiac).

Performance (Consul saloon)   Figures from "The Autocar" 15th November 1957

Max speed	77.5mph (mean), 80.6 (best)
2nd gear	58mph
1st gear	33mph
Acceleration	
0-60mph	25.4 seconds
$\frac{1}{4}$ mile	22.7 seconds

	Top gear	2nd gear
20-40mph	11.3 sec.	6.7 sec.
30-50mph	12.2 sec.	9.0 sec.
40-60mph	15.0 sec.	—
50-70mph	22.0 sec.	—
Fuel consumption	31.4mpg overall	

Performance (Zephyr Convertible)   Figures from "The Motor" 10th May 1961

Max speed	88.3mph (mean), 90.9 (best)
2nd gear	64mph
1st gear	37mph
Acceleration	
0-60mph	17.0 seconds
$\frac{1}{4}$ mile	20.6 seconds

	Top gear	2nd gear
20-40mph	8.0 sec.	4.8 sec.
30-50mph	8.8 sec.	5.6 sec.
40-60mph	10.2 sec.	9.0 sec.
50-70mph	14.4 sec.	—
Fuel consumption	22.1mpg overall	

Super Profile

The large window area combines well with the brightly coloured upholstery to give a pleasantly "airy" effect to the interior of WRR 167. The door locking button for the front door can just be seen on the door sill, both front doors can be locked/unlocked from the outside. The rear doors were locked by simply pushing the interior handle forward.

WRR 167 is an early 1957 Consul in original unrestored condition, fitted with the optional overriders and Ford accessory wing mirrors. The early model's high roof-line, in combination with the cut-back Consul fins and short four-cylinder engine compartment results in a quite compact-looking car from this angle.

The optional nylon-weave upholstery is featured in XTA 888, with the interior as a whole finished in tones complementary to the car's exterior in this case rather than the contrasting combinations which were also available.

The extended fins, and much longer bonnet of the six-cylinder cars gives a considerably longer look, which is exaggerated further on the Zodiacs by the straight two-tone division. This genuine low-mileage 1957 car has been fitted with later wheeltrims in more recent years, but is otherwise exactly as it left Dagenham.

Gold-plated script was an exclusive Zodiac feature which added to the luxury image of this car.

The optional radio fits neatly in the facia of XTA 888. The numerals on the early Mk2 instruments have a strange greenish, almost luminous appearance, and the instrument lighting is tinted slightly green, giving an almost eerie effect after dark.

The immaculate underbonnet scene of XTA 888, with only the modern white battery casing giving any hint that it is many years now since this car left Dagenham. The standard (pre Sept' 1960) Zodiac oil-bath air cleaner fills the front nearside corner.

The light-coloured roof of this De Luxe Consul helps to accentuate the low look. Compare the length of the four-cylinder car's front end with that of the Zodiac pictured earlier.

JSV 302

The slightly deeper screen introduced for the Low-Line models complements the flatter roof very well, and the additional brightwork adds some glamour to the Consul offsetting its rather plain grille. On all the Mk2s, the sidelamp units at the front incorporated white flashing direction indicators

The dark grey paintwork of this Low-Line Zephyr highlights the model's extensive brightwork to very good effect. The hooded headlamps and high centre bonnet line may not be as aerodynamic as some, but the Mk2 enthusiast just couldn't care less.

When in the raised position the convertible hood gives the car a slightly lower look than that of the saloons. The colour scheme chosen for this recently restored Zephyr suits the model particularly well, with the whitewall tyres adding the finishing touch to what many consider to be the most glamorous of all the big Fords.

And overdrive too – what a super car!

A beautifully original, unrestored Low-Line Zodiac automatic saloon, with only 16,000 miles on the clock and still running on its original whitewall tyres. In the centre of the hubcaps are genuine Ford accessory medallions which are themselves valued collectors items today.

The motif on the medallions is as on the steering wheel centre.

Front door armrests adjustable for height were exclusive to the Low-Line Zodiac.

A similar lever to that of the manual transmission cars is used to select the automatic drive. A wide brake pedal is provided to allow left-foot braking, and an organ type pedal matching the accelerator operates the headlamp dipping arrangements. The optional radio is styled into the lower panel, and alongside it can be seen the twist-release handbrake lever which replaced the pistol-grip ratchet lever of the pre Low-Line cars.

A somewhat more restrained colour scheme is displayed by this late-model Zodiac.

The standard leather upholstery of the Zodiac was more usually seen in dual tones, but single colours were available as depicted here. Despite more than 120,000 miles, the driver's seat shows no signs yet of beginning to sag. The seat belts are the genuine Ford accessory items which were available for the Mk2 cars during their production days.

ROAD TESTS

The Autocar
ROAD
TESTS

No. 1599

FORD
CONSUL
Mark II

Simplicity of line is maintained by the discreet use of chromium-plated mouldings. A single line along each side adds to the low look of the car. The radiator grille is plain but attractive, and the shape of front and rear wings helps the driver to place the car accurately. Overriders are available at extra cost

THERE is always a quickening of the motoring pulse when a new popular model appears from one of the really large manufacturers. Often it appears in such numbers and so quickly that, if it is handsome, the other cars in the popular field very soon begin to look out of date. The new Ford Consul, built beside the River Thames at Dagenham, already is being seen in numbers on roads throughout this country and abroad, and the traffic is enhanced by its presence.

Fords have achieved something rare in their design, because it is truly simple and well balanced, yet striking. Styling embellishment has been confined to a single moulding along each side, and even this helps to give a low appearance. The mildly finned shape of the wings at front and rear harmonizes with the general line of the model, and aids accurate placing of the car on the road. The Consul is obviously desirable for its appearance alone.

Another big change is the substantial increase in the interior dimensions. The earlier model would seat six in reasonable comfort on local journeys, but the new Consul is a six-seater in the full sense. Many threesomes will decide to sit together on the front seat for ease of conversation, as the driver still has plenty of room even for long journeys. A proportional increase has been made in the size of the luggage locker, which is of good depth as well as length and width. The spare wheel takes up a similar position to that used previously, and the counterbalancing mechanism for the lid is now covered in rubber for the protection of luggage. There is as much luggage space as the average family is likely to require.

When one enters the car, changes in the interior styling are seen to have effected a great improvement. The light-coloured upholstery is still of plastic, but buttoned to reduce any tendency to ripple. The seat cushion is surrounded by a second, darker colour which continues down to the base of the seats. Plastic, grained material is also used effectively on the top of the facia, in which the central ashtray has its metal treated to match. Plastic roof lining is now used instead of the fluffy cloth which quickly gets stained.

Good contemporary styling is characteristic also of the layout of the instruments. The speedometer, tucked under a raised cowl directly in front of the driver, is seen through the graceful, two-spoked wheel. Below it are the ammeter and fuel gauge, and indicator lights for oil pressure, main

beam, and the winking indicators which have replaced the semaphore type. (The indicators are now operated by an arm protruding from the right side of the steering column, which is pressed down for right, up for left, in accordance with the usual practice in this type of switch.)

The choke, lights and wiper switches are neatly placed below the instruments, with an additional, small toggle switch for the facia lighting. Between these is the ignition key, which also operates the starter. The key has four positions: to the left (anticlockwise) enables radio, lights, and so on, to be used; central turns everything off; right is the normal ignition-on position; and farther right, against a spring, operates the starter motor. This type of switch has been in use for some time on foreign cars and is a welcome fitting now in the popular field of British cars. The instrument layout has been arranged with thought, perhaps because it amounted to a fault on the earlier model. There is less shelf space on the Consul II, but a lockable glove compartment is incorporated on the passenger side.

The engine is similar in appearance to the smaller capacity unit used previously, but the heater is now mounted on the bulkhead. The battery, radiator cap and oil filler remain accessible, but the dipstick is still a little awkwardly placed on the opposite side from the carburettor —so low as to be out of view in this illustration

THE AUTOCAR, 15 JUNE 1956

An important change in styling is the incorporation of a wrap-round rear window, which blends well with the lines of the car as a whole. The locker lid opens by press-button and raises itself automatically. The fuel filler cap is behind the hinged number plate. The upper sections of the rear lights are coloured amber for the winking indicators, and below these are the tail and stop lights. Small circular reflectors also are fitted

FORD CONSUL . . .

Orthodox window winders and interior door handles have a smart shape. The car can now be locked or unlocked from either side, but it is not possible to lock all doors without a key. Floor covering is of moulded, light-coloured rubber at front and rear. Pendant clutch and brake pedals are accompanied by an organ-type throttle pedal. From the driver's point of view, a fault is that the steering wheel rim is near the seat, in a position in which it can limit his leg room severely.

The interior gives a light and airy impression which results from the colouring, slimmer windscreen pillars, and a great increase in rear window area. Visibility has been improved accordingly, and is now very good indeed. Full advantage has been taken of the wide rear window, in the use of a big rear mirror. This limits the view to some extent on certain types of left-hand bend and at some roundabouts, but the improvement in the rear view compensates for this minor fault, and the wide mirror is preferable to the curved type, which makes traffic appear farther away than it is.

It will be recalled that the engine of the new Consul is increased in size from 1,502 to 1,702 c.c. This has been accompanied by an increase of power from 47 to 59 b.h.p., and maximum torque is now 92 lb/ft at 2,300 r.p.m., compared with the previous 72 at 2,000 r.p.m. Although the unladen weight is increased only nominally, it might reasonably be thought that the larger car with its bigger engine would be greedy of fuel. However, there is, if anything, a slight improvement in the m.p.g. figures. Even mass-produced cars have their individual peculiarities, but in spite of allowing for these it may be assumed that the new model will achieve m.p.g. figures no worse than the earlier car.

The car tested gave, to be precise, 26.5 m.p.g. driven hard on British roads, and 33.8 driven quietly, cruising at about 40 m.p.h. with the carburettor governed by a light right foot. Thus Fords have achieved greatly increased space and better performance—as can be seen in the data—without ill effects on fuel consumption.

The liveliness of the engine is quickly evident. First gear runs the car smartly up to 20 to 25 m.p.h. without over-revving, and the middle ratio carries the speed

The simple grille is effective. The bumpers wrap well round, and the head lamps are attractively cowled. The side lights fulfil a dual role as winking indicators. The air intake for the heating system is at the base of the windscreen

on quickly to over a genuine 50 m.p.h. when required. Wind effects may have been responsible for a maximum speed that is not particularly impressive, but the car almost certainly would reach a true 80 m.p.h. in favourable circumstances.

More important is the capability of cruising at speeds well into the sixties without any suggestion of engine distress. Now that the capacity has been increased some roughness at low speed may be expected, but the compromise achieved by Ford's is justified by low cost production and maintenance. The minimum speed on top is not outstandingly low at 14 m.p.h., and below 25-30 m.p.h. the engine is not particularly smooth. However, at higher speeds there is no unreasonable roughness.

The noise level is satisfactorily low—that is it never becomes so obtrusive as to irritate occupants or cause conversation to be conducted in raised tones. Wind noise is also restrained when the windows are shut.

The transmission is outstanding in respect of the gear box. The car has only three speeds—which helps to simplify the arrangement of a steering-column gear change —and no synchromesh on first gear, but the change is so light and positive that it is just about as good as one which is controlled by a floor-mounted lever. With a three-speed box of this type, first gear must be used where often second would suffice on a four-speed box, and engagement of this gear on the move really demands the assistance of synchromesh action, to be entirely acceptable in 1956. However, double declutch changes are straightforward and the change up and down between second and top is superb. A change either way between the upper two gears can be achieved with the fingertips without taking a hand from the wheel. The proximity of first and reverse also aids manoeuvring.

The clutch pedal is placed too far from the floor, making it difficult to cover with the left foot in town driving without taking up the play. There is no axle noise, and gear noise is slight, even on the indirect ratios. Regardless of speed the transmission is free from vibration periods—a state of affairs not always found on the earlier model.

While praise is justifiably being directed at this model, it must be tempered with some qualification when the suspension and steering are reviewed. In normal motoring on a dry road there is a degree of understeer, but those who drive at a cracking pace will find some tendency to bumpskid at the rear, which can turn the understeer quickly into the opposite tendency. This is even more pronounced on wet roads where the change from under- to over-steer happens more suddenly, and where each characteristic is more pronounced.

For the normal owner the suspension is entirely satisfactory. It is firm without giving occupants a rough ride, it absorbs bumps at speed as if it was waiting for them, and the driver has a positive feel to his controls

The spare wheel is mounted to the right of the luggage locker, with hand tools tucked away beside it. The counterbalancing springs of the lid are covered in rubber

which is desirable. The most important improvement that could be made would be a reduction in the tendency for the rear wheels to hop on bump corners, as this—admittedly mild—effect is encountered even at low speeds when the surface is slippery and not quite smooth. The tyres run at 28 lb cold, which is somewhat high by present standards. This must have some effect on the axle top tendency at the rear. A size larger tyre at lower pressure might be used with advantage.

The steering itself has positive, light action. It has a modest 3¼ turns from lock to lock, and virtually no shock is felt at the wheel. The turning

FORD CONSUL SALOON Mark II

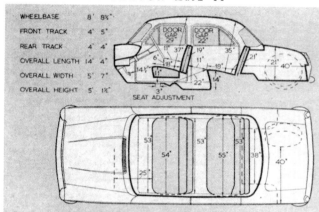

WHEELBASE	8' 8¾"
FRONT TRACK	4' 5"
REAR TRACK	4' 4"
OVERALL LENGTH	14' 4"
OVERALL WIDTH	5' 7"
OVERALL HEIGHT	5' 1¼"

Measurements in these ⅛in to 1ft scale body diagrams are taken with the driving seat in the central position of fore and aft adjustment and with the seat cushions uncompressed

PERFORMANCE

ACCELERATION: from constant speeds
Speed Range, Gear Ratios and Time in sec.

M.P.H.	4.11 to 1	6.75 to 1	11.67 to 1
10—30	—	—	6.3
20—40	11.35	6.9	—
30—50	12.7	8.7	—
40—60	16.5	—	—

From rest through gears to:

M.P.H.	sec.
30	6.4
50	15.85
60	25.0

Standing quarter mile, 23.1 sec.

SPEEDS ON GEARS:

Gear		M.P.H. (normal and max.)	K.P.H. (normal and max.)
Top	(mean)	75.2	120.9
	(best)	79	127.14
2nd		39—54	62.8—86.9
1st		20—28	32.2—45.1

TRACTIVE RESISTANCE: 47.5 lb per ton at 10 M.P.H.

TRACTIVE EFFORT:

	Pull (lb per ton)	Equivalent Gradient
Top	214.1	1 in 10.35
Second	344.1	1 in 6.58

BRAKES:

Efficiency	Pedal Pressure (lb)
35.5 per cent	25
62 per cent	50
72 per cent	75

FUEL CONSUMPTION:
29 m.p.g. overall for 540 miles (9.7 litres per 100 km).
Approximate normal range 26.5—33.8 m.p.g. (10.7—8.5 litres per 100 km).
Fuel, First grade.

WEATHER: Dry and sunny, light wind.
Air temperature 71 deg F.
Acceleration figures are the means of several runs in opposite directions.
Tractive effort and resistance obtained by Tapley meter.
Model described in *The Autocar* of March 2, 1956.

SPEEDOMETER CORRECTION: M.P.H.

Car speedometer:	10	20	30	40	50	60	70	75	76	80
True speed:	8	18	28	38	48	58	68	74	75	79

DATA

PRICE (basic), with saloon body, £520.
British purchase tax, £261 7s.
Total (in Great Britain), £781 7s.
Extras: Heater £14 5s.

ENGINE: Capacity: 1,703 c.c. (103.9 cu in).
Number of cylinders: 4.
Bore and stroke: 82.55 × 79.5 mm (3.25 × 3.13in).
Valve gear: o.h.v., pushrods.
Compression ratio: 7.8 to 1.
B.H.P.: 59 at 4,200 r.p.m. (B.H.P. per ton laden 47.2).
Torque: 92 lb ft at 2,300 r.p.m.
M.P.H. per 1,000 r.p.m. on top gear, 16.63.
WEIGHT: (with 5 gals fuel), 22 cwt (2,464 lb).
Weight distribution (per cent): F, 53.8; R, 46.2.
Laden as tested: 25 cwt (2,800 lb).
Lb per c.c. (laden): 1.6.
BRAKES: Type: Girling.
Method of operation: Hydraulic.
Drum dimensions: F, 9in diameter; 2¾in wide. R, 9in diameter; 1¾in wide.
Lining area: F, 86.48 sq in. R, 60.52 sq in (117.6 sq in per ton laden).
TYRES: 5.90—13in.
Pressures (lb per sq in): F, 28; R, 28 (normal).
TANK CAPACITY: 11 Imperial gallons.
Oil sump, 6 pints.
Cooling system, 18 pints (plus 1 pint if heater is fitted).
TURNING CIRCLE: 35ft. (L and R).
Steering wheel turns (lock to lock): 3¼.
DIMENSIONS: Wheelbase: 8ft 8¾in.
Track: F, 4ft 5in; R, 4ft 4in.
Length (overall): 14ft 4in.
Height: 5ft 1¼in.
Width: 5ft 7in.
Ground clearance: 6½in.
Frontal area: 22 sq ft (approximately).
ELECTRICAL SYSTEM: 12-volt; 45 ampère-hour battery.
Head lights: Double dip; 42—36 watt bulbs.
SUSPENSION: Front, Independent, coil springs, anti-roll bar. Rear, semi-elliptic.

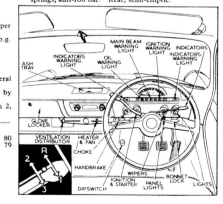

Entry to front and rear seats is simple and well suited to a family car. Two colours are used for the upholstery, and the seats are considerably wider than those of the earlier model. The siting of the instruments and minor controls is improved. A new shape has been adopted for window winders and door handles, and some shelf space has been sacrificed to a lockable glove compartment

FORD CONSUL . . .

circle has been improved, with the result that manœuvring in confined spaces is easier, but there is never any heaviness in its operation.

Braking power is good and no matter what driving technique is adopted there is never any trace of fade or any other undesirable phenomenon. Throughout the test the brakes remained smooth and free from grab. Free movement on the pedal was about the same at the end of the test as at the beginning. The hand-brake lever is of the customary pull-out type under the facia. A light pull is sufficient to hold the car firmly on steep hills, and the handle is situated so that it is easily reached on casual occasions such as brief halts in traffic on steep inclines.

The new model has a completely different horn from the earlier Consul's. It is an effective wind unit replacing the earlier "peep" of the cheaper, high-frequency component. It is a single Windtone, penetrating without being harsh. The lights are of the customary block pattern, with double dipping filaments. They are effective in the dipped position, but lack range for those who drive fast. At night the Consul is limited in speed by its lights, which do not do justice to the standard of the car's performance as a whole.

The car tested was fitted with the optionally extra heater, which has its controls installed below the facia. It was found that hot air could not be excluded entirely when the appropriate controls were set to cold. The intake is well placed just below the windscreen where it is not likely to pick up exhaust fumes from traffic, and interior heating and screen demisting are satisfactory so far as one could judge in the mild weather encountered during the test.

Ventilation provided by the windows is subject to criticism, however, as the swivelling windows in the front doors do not act with the extracting effect that is an important accomplishment of many windows of this type.

The filler for the fuel tank is unaccountably difficult to reach conveniently. It is neatly hidden behind the rear number plate, but the hinged plate will not swing right out of the way, so that the pump attendant must hold down the plate against a spring while filling the tank. This new Consul is attractive in its class as it offers so much room and performance, at a basic price, including purchase tax, of well under £800. It combines a handsome, modern appearance with technical improvements of real value. It has been designed with practical skill, and is likely to remain for a long time in the forefront of this country's "best buys."

It is offered in a wide range of colours which include two shades of blue, green, off-white and black, with two choices of interior colours for each shade. There are 16 grease nipples which require attention every 1,000 miles.

890   THE AUTOCAR, 14 DECEMBER 1956

Raymond Mays (left) and Peter Berthon, jointly responsible for this project, discuss the details with The Autocar artist, Vic Berris

RAYMOND MAYS CONVERSION

PROVIDES SPARKLING

ACCELERATION AND

OVER 100 m.p.h.

Below: The new cylinder head assembly ready for installation. The standard studs in the cylinder block are retained. Twin exhaust outlets require a new down pipe to complete the conversion

WHIRLWIND ZEPHYR

MORE and more cars are being placed on the market which can top a genuine 100 m.p.h., but too often at considerable sacrifice in acceleration in the intermediate range, or in handling qualities. The magic figure thus becomes an ultimate which is known to be latent, but which seldom can be attained in safety. Many special conversions for transforming standard models into high performance cars have been produced during the past few years, but the danger of " running out of chassis " becomes greater, because the basic design was never intended to meet such demands.

When the Ford Motor Company introduced the current range of Consul, Zephyr and Zodiac cars in March of this year, it was at once clear that the new models, although of considerably higher performance than their predecessors, had sufficient reserve in both mechanism and structure to cope with considerably greater power outputs. With the experience gained in producing their very successful conversion for the earlier-type Zephyr, the design staff of Rubery Owen Engine Development Division, in conjunction with Raymond Mays and Partners, of Bourne, in Lincolnshire, have

The secret of the car's performance is a very efficient b.m.e.p. curve which peaks at 154 lb sq in. Between 1,500 and 5,000 r.p.m. it is in excess of 130 lb sq in. Peak power of 127 b.h.p. with 8.75 to 1 compression ratio is 41 per cent higher than that of the standard Zephyr

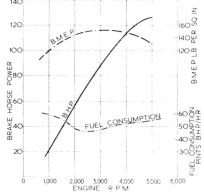

been quick to develop the new car in like fashion.

During many months of bench-testing, no modifications were found necessary below the cylinder head, the standard pistons, connecting rods, crankshaft and bearings proving fully equal to an even greater increase in power output than is claimed for the conversion under review. The extra power has been achieved with a new light alloy cylinder head having a separate inlet port to each combustion chamber; to these is matched a light alloy inlet manifold fed by two S.U. H.4 semi-downdraught carburettors. There are two cast iron exhaust manifolds each leading from three cylinder outlets, and the pipes leading from them are joined before entering a single Servais silencer.

The head is cast in aluminium alloy, and has austenitic cast iron valve seats shrunk in. It carries larger than standard inlet valves of Silchrome, and exhausts of XB alloy steel. As in the original engine, single valve springs are fitted, but they are somewhat stronger to cope with the extra stresses imposed by the larger valves and higher crankshaft speeds. The Ford valve stem synthetic seals are retained.

The induction manifold is a single casting, plugged midway along the main gallery, but having a small drilling to maintain balance. The manifold is tubular in cross-section, and its two inlets from the carburettors and six outlets to the head are arranged at 45 deg. A hollow well of square section is cast into the under surface of each " half," the

wells receiving heat direct from the exhaust manifolds. Thus any raw fuel collecting in these hot-spots is vaporized.

Two compression ratios are offered; the lower, 8.75 to 1, enables the engine to be run on premium fuels, but the higher, 9.2 to 1, requires 100 octane fuels if pinking is to be avoided. The claimed output with the 8.75 ratio is 127 b.h.p. (gross), and with the 9.2 ratio, 132 b.h.p. For racing a special camshaft has been evolved to increase the output to about 145 b.h.p., and the 2.6 litre Zephyr engine appears to take even this boost in its stride.

With the lower compression ratio, a maximum torque figure of 154 lb ft is produced at 3,000 r.p.m., and the b.h.p. figures quoted are achieved at 4,750 r.p.m. Above this crankshaft speed, however, torque is well maintained, and recommended peak revs are about 5,200-5,500 r.p.m. During development work a speed of 6,200 r.p.m. was found quite feasible. Comparative figures for the standard product with 7.8 to 1 compression are 90 b.h.p. at 4,400 r.p.m. and maximum torque of 137 lb ft at 2,000 r.p.m.

The only chassis modifications suggested are the fitting at the rear of Armstrong Silverstone-type dampers which have been specially developed for use on this car, and perhaps harder brake linings to resist fade during repeated hard applications from high speeds. It goes almost without saying that the Borg Warner overdrive, which is a standard extra for the Zephyr, becomes even more

Super Profile

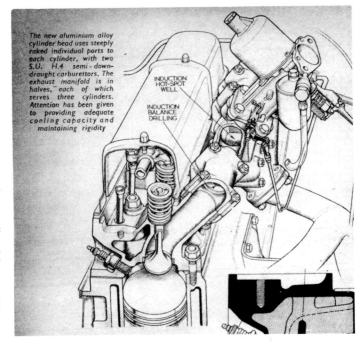

The installation calls for no major chassis alterations or redisposition of existing components

of an asset with this more powerful engine.

In the car submitted for trial, the 9.2 compression ratio was used, with overdrive, and a Consul final drive ratio of 4.1 to 1 replaced the normal Zephyr's 3.9. The latter increases accelerative powers in all ratios at the cost of negligible reduction in the maximum speeds, and allows overdrive top to be used more profitably. At 5,500 r.p.m. the equivalent road speed in normal top with this ratio is 97 m.p.h., and at 4,000 r.p.m. in overdrive top the car is travelling at 101.2 m.p.h. Thus it will be seen that the converted Zephyr could be cruised at this speed indefinitely on suitable Continental highways, without the engine approaching peak revs—an achievement for a car which costs little over £1,000 when modified to this standard.

During our tests a true maximum of over 100 m.p.h. in overdrive top was recorded in both directions over a limited distance, and it seems that, with a greater distance in which to gather speed, the level maximum might well be about 105 m.p.h.

Although this figure is impressive, the most significant feature of the car's performance is its quite exceptional acceleration through the gears in direct drive, when a true 90 m.p.h. can be reached from a standing start in about 25 sec. This places the Raymond Mays Zephyr well in the lead for sheer performance before any other five-six-seater British saloon, and its acceleration figures are even superior to those of some sports cars with considerably larger engines, and costing several times as much.

Taking some advantage of the Zephyr's potentialities, but not driving it to the limit except for an occasional burst of speed where the opportunity occurred, the fuel consumption was 22 m.p.g. Really hard driving naturally takes its toll, but comparative figures for standard and converted cars at equivalent speeds show even a slight credit for the tuned version. Although the exhaust note on this hotter version is a little louder and crisper than normal, it has no sporting bark or crackle, and never becomes obtrusive.

Enhanced performance could well be more of a liability than an asset, were the Ford chassis not up to the mark, but at no time did it show any shortcomings in steering or road-holding. Nor did the brakes fade during a considerable mileage covered in the hands of several members of *The Autocar* staff, though repeated hard use of them during high-speed

driving might have induced it, and the prospective owner would be advised to have harder linings than standard fitted.

A criticism of the car tested was that the throttle linkage geometry was poorly arranged, in that the throttles were opened too rapidly on initial slight depression of the accelerator pedal. This made it difficult to move off the mark other than rather violently, which sometimes proved a little embarrassing in heavy traffic. We understand, however, that this matter is appreciated at Bourne, and is receiving attention.

Starting, hot or cold, was straightforward and infallible—in fact, little or no use of the choke control was called for, even on quite a cold morning. The carburettor settings on the car tried were a little uneven for good slow running, and at low speeds the mixture seemed a little over-rich. Nevertheless, the car was

tractable enough, if one discounted the irritation of that throttle linkage. On 100 octane fuel there was sometimes a momentary trace of pinking when one changed from overdrive into direct drive by the full throttle kick-down method.

We were also able to take Mr. Mays' own Zephyr for a brief run. It has the 8.75 compression ratio, which does not demand 100 octane petrol, and is slightly smoother and more tractable, with very little reduction in power at the wheels. It is, in fact, every bit as smooth as the standard product.

At £135 (without fitting) this modification will have a great appeal to enthusiasts, especially those who use their cars for competitive motoring in long-distance Continental rallies. It seems ideal also for those whose business or pleasure carries them far afield on very fast roads.

It is difficult to think of many more standard family saloons which would lend themselves so readily to this sort of development, so that the Ford Motor Company must take a large proportion of the credit for providing such a fine basis. Those at Bourne have been quick to appreciate these qualities, and have taken the trouble painstakingly to develop this really worth-while conversion set.

PERFORMANCE FIGURES

Mean max. speed .. .. 101 m.p.h. (limited run)

Acceleration M.P.H.	sec.
0—30	3.3
0—50	7.5
0—60	10.0
0—70	14.5
0—80	19.3
0—90	25.5

Standing ¼-mile 17.6 secs.

The new aluminium alloy cylinder head uses steeply raked individual ports to each cylinder, with two S.U. H.4 semi-down-draught carburettors. The exhaust manifold is in halves, each of which serves three cylinders. Attention has been given to providing adequate cooling capacity and maintaining rigidity

The Motor   904   *January 2, 1957*

The Motor Road Test No. 1/57 ——

Make: Ford.   **Type:** Zodiac II with Borg-Warner Automatic Transmission

Makers: The Ford Motor Co. Ltd., Dagenham, Essex.

Test Data

CONDITIONS: Weather: Cool, dry, light breeze. (Temperature 48°/49°F., Barometer 30.1/30.2 in. Hg.), Surface: Smooth tar macadam. Fuel: Premium grade pump petrol, approx. 95 Research Method Octane Rating.

INSTRUMENTS

Speedometer at 30 m.p.h.	.. ..	1"₃ fast
Speedometer at 60 m.p.h.	.. ..	accurate
Speedometer at 80 m.p.h.	.. ..	accurate
Distance recorder	.. ..	2"₀ fast

WEIGHT

Kerb weight (unladen, but with oil, coolant and fuel for approx. 50 miles) 25½ cwt.
Front/rear distribution of kerb weight   58/42
Weight laden as tested   .   ..   ..   29 cwt.

MAXIMUM SPEEDS

Flying Quarter Mile

Not recorded (owing to current fuel difficulties).

"Maximile" Speed (Timed quarter mile after one mile accelerating from rest).
Mean of four opposite runs   ..   83.1 m.p.h.
Best one-way time equals   ..   85.7 m.p.h.

Speed in Gears

Max. speed in intermediate gear   ..   55 m.p.h.
Max. speed in low gear   ..   ..   30 m.p.h.

FUEL CONSUMPTION

31½ m.p.g. at constant 30 m.p.h. on level.
28   m.p.g. at constant 40 m.p.h. on level.
25¼ m.p.g. at constant 50 m.p.h. on level.
23   m.p.g. at constant 60 m.p.h. on level.
17½ m.p.g. at constant 70 m.p.h. on level.

Overall Fuel Consumption for 594.8 miles, 28.5 gallons, equals 20.9 m.p.g. (13.5 litres/100 km.).

Touring Fuel Consumption (m.p.g. at steady speed midway between 30 m.p.h. and maximum, less 5%₀ allowance for acceleration), 22.6 m.p.g.

Fuel Tank Capacity (maker's figure)   10½ gal.

STEERING

Turning circle between kerbs :
   Left   ..   ..   36¾ feet
   Right   ..   ..   34¼ feet
Turns of steering wheel from lock to lock 3½

BRAKES from 30 m.p.h.

0.86g retardation (equivalent to 35 ft. stopping distance) with 105 lb. pedal pressure
0.84g retardation (equivalent to 36 ft. stopping distance) with 75 lb. pedal pressure
0.64g retardation (equivalent to 47 ft. stopping distance) with 50 lb. pedal pressure
0.29g retardation (equivalent to 103 ft. stopping distance) with 25 lb. pedal pressure

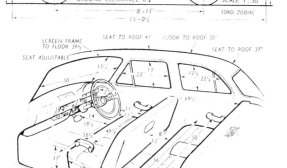

FRONT 4'-5"   TRACK   REAR 4'-4"   OVERALL WIDTH 5'-8¾"

5'-2   GROUND CLEARANCE 6¼"   SCALE 1 : 50   FORD ZODIAC   8'-11"   15'-0½"

SCREEN FRAME TO FLOOR 39½"   SEAT TO ROOF 41"   FLOOR TO ROOF 50"   SEAT TO ROOF 37"

SEAT ADJUSTABLE   NOT TO SCALE   FRONT DOOR   REAR DOOR

ACCELERATION TIMES from Standstill (kick-down condition).

0-30 m.p.h.	..	..	5.9 sec.
0-40 m.p.h.	..	..	9.2 sec.
0-50 m.p.h.	..	..	12.5 sec.
0-60 m.p.h.	..	..	17.4 sec.
0-70 m.p.h.	..	..	27.0 sec.
0-80 m.p.h.	..	..	39.9 sec.
Standing quarter mile	..	..	22.3 sec.

ACCELERATION TIMES In Drive Range

			Top gear	Kick-down condition
0-20 m.p.h.	..	..	—	3.3 sec.
10-30 m.p.h.	..	..	—	4.3 sec.
20-40 m.p.h.	..	..	—	5.9 sec.
30-50 m.p.h.	..	..	9.3 sec.	6.6 sec.
40-60 m.p.h.	..	..	11.1 sec.	8.2 sec.
50-70 m.p.h.	..	..	15.2 sec.	14.5 sec.
60-80 m.p.h.	..	..	22.5 sec.	22.5 sec.

HILL CLIMBING at sustained steady speeds

Max. gradient on top gear   ..   1 in 10.8 (Tapley 205 lb./ton)
Max. gradient on intermediate gear   ..   1 in 6.8 (Tapley 325 lb./ton)

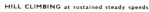

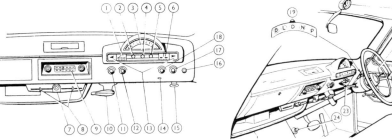

1. Fuel contents gauge. 2. Oil pressure warning light. 3. Speedometer. 4. Headlamp main beam warning light. 5. Dynamo charge warning light. 6. Ammeter. 7. Cigar lighter. 8. Heater controls. 9. Radio (optional extra). 10. Handbrake. 11. Ignition key and starter switch. 12. Choke. 13. Direction indicator warning lamps. 14. Instrument lighting switch. 15. Bonnet release. 16. Windscreen washer switch. 17. Windscreen wiper control. 18. Head and sidelight switch. 19. Transmission selector quadrant. 20. Clock. 21. Direction indicator switch. 22. Horn ring. 23. Transmission selector lever. 24. Headlamp dip-switch.

B6

January 2, 1957   905   *THE MOTOR*

—The FORD ZODIAC II

(With Automatic Transmission)

Low, wide and handsome, the Zodiac has liveliness to match. Addition of the Borg-Warner transmission contributes to simple and restful driving; the relative positions of the brake and accelerator pedals *(below)* permit the country dweller wearing outsize boots to retain full control at all times.

Borg-Warner Torque Converter System Blends Well With Dagenham's Lively 2½-litre Six-seater

AUTOMATIC transmissions embodying torque converters have become immensely popular in the United States since the war. There, of course, engines of four and five litres are normal and, until recently, there has been a widespread idea that this type of transmission is inherently unsuitable for use with the medium and small engine sizes common in this country. At the Earls Court Show last autumn, however, several British cars of 2½-litres were offered for the first time with automatic torque-converter transmissions and particular interest attaches to the car reviewed in this road test report as being the first such model to be tested by *The Motor*.

Far from being unsuitable, the Ford Zodiac II and the Borg-Warner automatic transmission form a particularly happy combination. The Zodiac II is a lively car and a roomy one. The automatic transmission makes it a very restful vehicle as well.

The system used follows the normal Borg-Warner practice, with a torque converter working in conjunction with an automatically-operated three-speed-and-reverse epicyclic gearbox. There is no clutch pedal and once the appropriate position has been selected by means of a neat steering-column control lever, progress is regulated entirely by the accelerator and brake.

Five positions are provided for the control level. There are two neutrals, in one of which (labelled "P" for Park) the transmission is locked so that the car will not move, even if the handbrake is not applied. Two forward positions are also provided, "D" (for Drive) giving the automatic range and being used for all normal purposes, whilst the other, labelled "L" (for Low) retains the transmission in low gear for descending steep hills; adjacent to it is "R," giving reverse gear.

In order to avoid accidental engagement of Low or Reverse by overshooting Drive, the lever has to be lifted slightly against a light spring pressure and a similar movement is necessary to engage the parking pawl.

In the drive range, the car moves off immediately the accelerator is depressed and the transmission passes progressively through low and intermediate gears into top as the road speed rises. Changes do not, however, take place at set speeds, the actual changing points being dependent upon throttle opening. Thus, the change from bottom to intermediate on the Zodiac occurs at about 10 m.p.h. if the throttle is opened only lightly, but is delayed to 18 m.p.h. if the throttle is fully opened; similarly, the change from intermediate to top varies from 20 m.p.h. as a minimum to 33 m.p.h. as a normal maximum.

The qualification "normal" is important because a further feature is the kick-down

In Brief

Price (including Borg-Warner automatic transmission as tested): £770 plus purchase tax £386 7s. 0d. equals £1,156 7s. 0d.

Price with normal transmission (including purchase tax) £968 17s. 0d.

Capacity	2,553 c.c.
Unladen kerb weight ...	25½ cwt.
Acceleration:	
20-40 m.p.h. in drive range	5.9 sec.
0-50 m.p.h. through gears	12.5 sec.
Maximum direct top gear gradient	1 in 10.8

Maximum speed: Not recorded owing to current fuel difficulties.

Maximile speed	83.1 m.p.h.
Touring fuel consumption ...	22.6 m.p.g.

Gearing: 18.9 m.p.h. in top gear at 1,000 r.p.m. 36.2 m.p.h. at 1,000 ft./min. piston speed.

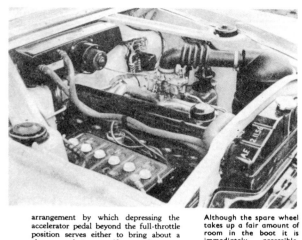

THE MOTOR 906 *January 2, 1957*

The FORD ZODIAC II

Grouped around a long, neat-looking engine are the battery (on the opposite side to the exhaust manifold), a very efficient Smiths heater tailored to fit the scuttle pressing, windscreen washer reservoir, and carburetter air filter and intake. Struts reinforce the top mountings of the i.f.s.

arrangement by which depressing the accelerator pedal beyond the full-throttle position serves either to bring about a change to a lower gear, if appropriate, or to delay engagement of the next higher gear. Thus, when taking off from rest, the change from bottom to intermediate may be delayed until 30 m.p.h. is reached and the subsequent change into top postponed to 55 m.p.h., the kick-down arrangement also being available if it is desired to revert to a lower gear for added power.

The speed ranges chosen suit the characteristics of the Zodiac extremely well and provide for all normal driving conditions in a particularly happy manner. The take-off is smooth although, as with most automatic transmissions, the driver has a sense of slightly less delicate control when "edging" the car in confined spaces. It is worth remembering, however, that the left foot can always be used on the double-width brake pedal in such circumstances and, indeed, this practice works particularly well because the natural instinct of a driver accustomed to a normal transmission is to press down his "clutch" foot to restrain movement.

Both upward and downward changes take place very unobtrusively although, with a wide-open throttle, the car makes a smooth but perceptible bound forward as a higher gear engages, owing to the inertia of the engine. When the object is to accelerate as rapidly as possible, this is satisfying rather than otherwise, but it is

Although the spare wheel takes up a fair amount of room in the boot it is immediately accessible, and the remaining space can accommodate a considerable amount of bulky luggage. The fuel filler is concealed behind the spring-loaded number plate.

slightly annoying when a driver wishes to ease up after accelerating hard in intermediate (as when overtaking one car of a queue and slipping into a gap). Another slight criticism is that the kick-down action was rather stiff and a short but appreciable time lag occurred before the actual change took place.

In writing of any automatic transmission, however, one must stress that the standards of the expert driver who is capable of getting the best out of a normal clutch and gearbox are not those of a driver of only average skill. To the latter, what the expert may regard as minor shortcomings literally do not exist because the results produced are as good as, or better than, the best he can achieve. Thus, to the expert, the Borg-Warner can occasionally cause slight irritation by an unwanted change into a higher gear when the throttle is momentarily eased, but, in the main, the change control mechanism is not annoyingly oversensitive.

During the course of the test, we carried out a number of restarts on a 1 in 4 gradient (two up) with the greatest of ease (the only fault showing up being the feebleness of the handbrake) and another test was a 4 m.p.h. climb of a moderately steep hill over half a mile in length to see whether the torque converter had any objections to prolonged crawling under load; it had not. Both bottom and intermediate gears, incidentally, are commendably quiet.

Inevitably, a transmission such as this adds some weight and absorbs some power, and it is in these respects that the wisdom of applying such a system to a medium-powered car has sometimes been queried. It is interesting, therefore, to find that comparisons between the present test and one carried out on a similar Zodiac model with normal transmission last year (vide *The Motor*, May 2, 1956) show that the performance differences are of a very minor order.

In the important matter of fuel consumption, for example, m.p.g. figures at various constant speeds from 30 m.p.h. upwards were mostly so close as to have little significance. At 50 m.p.h., in fact, the two were identical. These results were reinforced by the overall fuel consumption check which showed 20.9 m.p.g. for the automatic transmission model compared with 21.5 m.p.g. for the normal-gearbox type. Undoubtedly a point affecting this is the fact that the Borg-Warner transmission is arranged to provide a direct (positive) drive in top gear.

Acceleration times from a standstill through the gears show a slight increase with 12.5 seconds to 50 m.p.h. compared with 11.3 seconds, and 39.9 seconds to 80 m.p.h. compared with 37.8 seconds. In

Easy to enter or leave through four wide, front-hinged doors, the Zodiac is a roomy car with particularly ample legroom in the rear. The rear seat has a folding centre armrest which could well be duplicated in the front.

(With Automatic Transmission)

this case, however, it must be emphasized that the figures recorded for the Borg-Warner model could be matched by *any* driver, whereas those recorded with the ordinary gearbox represent the performances of two skilful drivers losing the absolute minimum time on the gear changes.

As can be seen from the photographs and diagrams, the instruments and controls generally are arranged in a logical and convenient manner, but the position of the brake pedal in relation to the accelerator called for adverse comment by some who drove the car, the brake pedal being 5 inches nearer the driving seat than the accelerator.

Although the arc-type speedometer is nicely in front of the driver it had a minor fault at night in that light from the indirect illumination escaped to the roof where, whilst not causing any serious distraction, it did create the irritating illusion of a following car. The instruments, too, are rather austere.

As has already been indicated, the Zodiac is a very roomy car and the seats themselves are comfortable, the rear in particular providing unusually generous leg room. A very surprising omission is the absence of a central armrest in the front. Side armrests are provided on the doors, but as these are non-adjustable they suit only a proportion of users.

Vision is unusually good all round and all wings, front and rear, can be seen from the driving seat, making it particularly easy to place the car and to manoeuvre in confined spaces. Entry and exit is easy at both front and rear, and both front doors can be locked from the outside by a key or from the inside by pulling up a plunger.

Exceptionally good all-round visibility is a feature of the new Fords, the wrap-around rear window contributing largely to this.

The rear boot provides good accommodation and there is a moderate-size parcel shelf and a rather small cubby locker inside the body, but storage for odds and ends could be increased with advantage by the provision of door pockets. The interior heater is efficient and its controls are above average in permitting accurate regulation without over-finicky adjustment. Another exceptionally good feature is the interior light which is located on the near-side door pillar and has a plastics cover in which a lens is moulded. The result is illumination over the whole interior, plus a concentrated beam for map-reading.

The engine is smooth, willing, and, in the main, unobtrusive, although some slight degree of "power roar" is present at 60 m.p.h. upwards, whilst one has the feeling that the unit is working rather hard if taken to its "kick-down" limit. Starting on cold mornings calls for a fairly precise manipulation of controls because the normal fast idle for warming-up is deliberately limited to avoid the car creeping unduly in gear. Thus a little juggling is necessary to steer between stalling due to over-richness and the same result due to a slow idle on a lean mixture.

Steering is only slightly heavier due to the extra weight of an automatic transmission at the front of the car and, although the car has not quite so much "feel" as some, cornering qualities are good, with very little roll at touring speeds, whilst an accurate course is followed with no appreciable over/understeer to disconcert the driver. With moderately firm suspension, the general standards of road holding and comfort are also very satisfactory.

In all, this latest Zodiac II with automatic transmission forms a very happy combination which will appeal strongly to all who require a roomy car of notably good appearance, distinctly brisk performance, and a transmission which completely solves gear-changing problems for the poor or moderate driver and provides a very restful way of motoring for the expert.

Specification

Engine

Cylinders	6
Bore	82.55 mm.
Stroke	79.5 mm.
Cubic capacity	2,553 c.c.
Piston area	49.79 sq. in.
Valves	Inclined o.h.v. (push rods)
Compresson ratio	7.8/1
	(6.9/1 optional for poor fuels)
Carburetter	Zenith 36 mm. downdraught
Fuel pump	AC Delco mechanical
Ignition timing control	Centrifugal and vacuum
Oil filter	Full-flow
Max. power	90 b.h.p.
	(86 b.h.p. with low compression)
at	4,400 r.p.m.
Piston speed at max. b.h.p.	2,300 ft./min.

Transmission

Borg-Warner automatic transmission (incorporating torque converter).

Top gear	3.9 (direct drive)
Intermediate	5.596
	(11.19 with max. torque multiplication)
Low	8.981
	(17.96 with max. torque multiplication)
Reverse	7.835
	(15.67 with max. torque multiplication)
Propeller shaft	Open Hardy Spicer
Final drive	Hypoid bevel
Top gear m.p.h at 1,000 r.p.m.	18.9
Top gear m.p.h. at 1,000 ft./min. piston speed	36.2

Chassis

Brakes	Girling hydraulic (2 l.s. on front)
Brake drum internal diameter	9 in.
Friction lining area	147 sq. in.
Suspension:	
Front	Independent (directly operated coil springs with anti-roll bar)
Rear	Semi-elliptic
Shock absorbers:	
Front	Telescopic hydraulic
Rear	Lever-arm hydraulic
Steering gear	Worm and peg
Tyres	6.70—13 (4-ply)

Coachwork and Equipment

Starting handle	Nil
Battery mounting	Under bonnet on r.h. side
Jack	Bipod type
Jacking points	One below body sill on each side
Standard tool kit:	Jack, wheelbrace, grease gun, pliers, three screwdrivers (one for Phillips screws), adjustable wrench, two double-ended open spanners, two double-ended box spanners, combined tommy bar and drain-plug key, two tyre levers.
Exterior lights:	Two headlamps, two side/flasher lamps, two stop/tail/flasher lamp clusters, two rear number plate lamps.
Number of electrical fuses	Four
Direction indicators	Flasher type, self cancelling
Windscreen wipers	Twin-blade vacuum type, self-parking, with vacuum pump
Windscreen washers	Twin-jet vacuum type
Sun vizors	Two
Instruments:	Speedometer (with decimal mileage recorder but no trip), fuel gauge, ammeter, clock.

Warning lights:	Dynamo charge, oil pressure, direction indicators and headlamp main beam.
Locks:	
With ignition key	Front doors, glove locker and rear boot
With other keys	Nil
Glove lockers	One on passenger's side
Map pockets	None
Parcel shelves	Under glove locker and behind rear seat
Ashtrays	One front, one rear
Cigar lighters	One on facia panel
Interior lights	One on centre door pillar (with courtesy switches)
Interior heater:	Fresh-air type heater and de-mister (with intake below windscreen).
Extras available	Radio
Upholstery material	Leather on wearing surfaces, P.V.C. elsewhere
Floor covering	Pile carpet
Exterior colours standardized:	Six two-tone combinations and eight single colours.
Alternative body styles	Convertible

Maintenance

Sump: 7 pints S.A.E. 20 (summer and winter)
Automatic gearbox: 15 pints special automatic transmission fluid (e.g. Castrol TQ automatic transmission fluid, Type A).
Rear axle ... 2.5 pints S.A.E. 90 E.P. (summer and winter)
Steering gear lubricant Extreme pressure oil (0.68 pints)
Cooling system capacity ... 22 pints (one drain tap)
Chassis lubrication By grease gun every 1,000 miles to 14 points
Ignition timing: 8° b.t.d.c. (high compression); 4° b.t.d.c. (low compression).
Spark plug type ... Champion N8B
Spark plug gap ... 0.032 in.

Contact breaker gap 0.014/0.016 in.
Valve timing: Inlet opens 17° b.t.d.c. and closes 51° a.b.d.c.; exhaust opens 49° b.b.d.c. and closes 19° a.t.d.c.

Tappet clearances (hot):	
Inlet	0.014 in.
Exhaust	0.014 in.
Front wheel toe-in	$\frac{1}{8}$-$\frac{1}{4}$ in.
Camber angle	+1$\frac{1}{4}$-+2$\frac{1}{4}$°
Castor angle	-$\frac{1}{4}$-+1$\frac{1}{4}$°
Steering swivel pin inclination	+3$\frac{1}{4}$-+4$\frac{1}{4}$°
Tyre pressures:	
Front	24 lb.
Rear	24 lb.
Brake fluid	EnFo brake fluid
Battery type and capacity	12-volt, 57 amp./hr.

466

THE AUTOCAR, 18 MARCH 1960

USED CARS on the Road

No. 154—1957 FORD CONSUL II CONVERTIBLE

PRICES: Secondhand £695; New—basic £630, with tax £946

Acceleration from rest through gears:

to 30 m.p.h.	6.9 sec	20 to 40 m.p.h. (top gear)	9.9 sec
to 50 m.p.h.	14.5 sec	30 to 50 m.p.h. (top gear)	11.7 sec
to 60 m.p.h.	22.6 sec	*Standing quarter-mile*	21.8 sec

Petrol consumption	21-28 m.p.g.
Oil consumption	negligible
Mileometer reading	35,570
Date first registered	1 February 1957

Provided for test by L. F. Dove, Ltd., Austin House, 111-115, Addiscombe Road, East Croydon, Surrey. Telephone: Addiscombe 3066.

Draught sealing with the hood in position is reasonable but not perfect. The shape of the Consul is particularly attractive in its convertible form. There are, of course, only two doors; the backrest of the front bench seat is divided, and folds forwards to give access to the rear compartment

CONVERTIBLES are something of an anomaly on the used car market. When they are new their prices are a great deal higher than for the corresponding saloon, primarily because they are produced in limited quantities. When they are a few years old, however, demand for them as used cars is lower than for equivalent saloons, and the question arises: to what should the price be related—the original cost when new, or the retail demand? This early-1957 Ford Consul convertible is offered at a price considerably higher than would be asked for equivalent Consul saloons, but a difference of £145, when it was purchased new, should be taken into consideration.

Power-operated hoods were available at extra cost for the Consul, but the example tested had the normal manually operated mechanism. It proved very simple to lower the hood, by first releasing the side supports and folding it back to the intermediate *coupé de ville* position, and then, releasing a catch below the edge of the rear seat, pushing it down into its well. The hood stows completely out of sight, and when it is lowered the tonneau cover conceals it quickly and reasonably tidily, although some of its spring clip fastenings are missing. The hood itself is clean externally, but inside there are many stains where dampness, seeping through, has marked the lining. In the raised position the hood gives rise to many rattles.

Yellow paintwork is used for the exterior finish, and although unattractive to some tastes, it blends quite well with the shape of the Consul convertible. A small dent in the luggage locker lid, and one or two shallow scratches, have been retouched with a poorly matching colour, but the general appearance of the paintwork is good. Rust is confined to the edges of the window slots in the doors, and to some parts of the door surrounds. The chromium shows little sign of deterioration except on the rear bumper, which at some time has been bent in the middle.

Evidence of extensive use is seen inside the car: the floor carpets in both front and rear compartments are well worn, and the front bench seat has sagged appreciably on the driver's side. The grey leather upholstery is slightly creased but sound, and the majority of the interior metalwork is unmarked.

At idling speeds a mild degree of piston slap is audible from the engine, and fumes are smelt sometimes inside the car. Wear is to be expected, but the willing performance of the power unit, its small oil consumption and the commendably low level of engine noise inside the car—even at high speed—together imply that a considerable lease of life remains ahead of it. This cannot be said of the clutch, which is in a poor state. Clutch spin occurs even in unhurried gear changes, and it can be provoked even by accelerating hard when the car is climbing uphill in top gear. As the pedal is in correct adjustment the need for a replacement unit is indicated, and it is understood from L. F. Dove that this is to be attended to before the car is sold.

Well-suited to the character of the Consul is its three-speed gearbox with steering column gear change which is pleasantly precise and light to operate. The synchromesh is effective on the two upper gears, and the unsynchronized bottom gear is readily engaged while on the move by double-declutching.

Very light steering is a feature of the Consul, yet it is not excessively low-geared, and quite pleasant control of the car is provided. No detectable free play has developed; there is no feed back of road shocks through the steering, and the directional stability of the car is particularly good. Even in a strong cross-wind a light hold on the wheel is adequate to keep the Consul straight.

Slight weakening of the suspension dampers is noticed when the car is driven fast over an undulating surface, but a very comfortable ride remains one of the best attributes of the car. Roadholding is extremely good, and the Consul corners fast with little roll and negligible tyre squeal; in hard driving on winding roads the car remains easy to control, and its behaviour is entirely predictable. The understeer tendency is scarcely noticed, and the car never seems unwilling to follow the chosen line.

When the car was received for test the brakes—although working satisfactorily—were in serious need of adjustment, indicated by the embarrassingly long pedal travel. This was rectified by our own service garage at the beginning of the test mileage. The hand brake is powerful and convenient to use. Another fault is that a new thermostat is needed. Until practically the whole of the radiator had been blanked off, the engine was running far too cold.

Some corrosion was noticed around the battery, but it did not lack power. Accessories of the Consul comprise a fresh-air heater (of which the controls are out of adjustment), small spot and flat beam auxiliary lamps, a windscreen washer and two exterior mirrors. Rust has affected the springs of the outside mirrors, and the interior one also lacks rigidity. The effect of all three mirrors wobbling on their supports is disconcerting.

A radio aerial is still fitted to the car, but the radio itself has been removed by a previous owner and an unsightly metal plate now covers the space which it occupied in the facia.

All but one of the tyres are remoulds, and three are nearly due for replacement; the other two are approximately a third worn. The toolkit is complete, and comprises a jack, wheelbrace and a few hand tools.

Referring again to the question of value which was discussed in the first paragraph, it is clear with this Consul that the price is related—more than anything else—to the original cost when new. At a fraction under £700 the price now asked for the car represents a depreciation rate of some £80 per year, and it may be questioned whether this compensates fully for the deterioration which has occurred.

Instruments of the Consul comprise a steady and commendably accurate speedometer with total mileometer (no trip), an ammeter and fuel gauge. All the electrical and mechanical equipment is working efficiently, and the suction-operated windscreen wipers (with pump assistance) are not unduly affected by variations in engine speed and load

68

Ford Zephyr

WITH DISC BRAKES

Minor bodywork changes on the Zephyr, made two years ago, included a flatter roof pressing and the use of stainless steel for screen and rear window surrounds

APPROXIMATELY five years of continuous production have served to strengthen the esteem in which the Series II Ford Zephyr is held in many parts of the world. Detail changes and improvements have been made during that time, and, as described in *The Autocar* 30 September, 1960, Girling disc front brakes may now be obtained as initial equipment at extra cost; they were fitted to the example submitted for test.

Since a Zephyr was last tested (described in *The Autocar* 2 August 1957) several bodywork changes have been made. The domed roof pressing is flatter, which has improved appearance though leaving virtually the same headroom; this is ample for both front and rear seat occupants. Instruments have been re-grouped beneath a rectangular cowl high up on the facia, where they can be examined with the minimum deviation of the eyes from the line of sight when driving. The speedometer now has a horizontal scale with no sub-divisions between the 10 m.p.h. increments; on the test car it read 10 m.p.h. fast at maximum speed. Other instruments, comprising fuel gauge and water thermometer, are immediately beneath it. There is a mileage recorder but no trip mileometer.

Safety padding along the upper edge of the facia is of suitable firmness to offer good protection from injury, and the top surface has a covering of dark-coloured grained plastic which effectively stops reflections from sun or street lighting. This is not true of the half horn ring on the dished, two-spoke steering wheel, the arms of the ring presenting quite large areas of bright chromium plating at such an angle that the sun reflecting in them can dazzle the driver. The horns are very powerful, with rather strident notes. It was found that this half ring was not always very easy to reach quickly for sounding the horns, because of its changing position as the wheel was turned.

Driver's visibility is first class in the Zephyr. Screen pillars are slender and raked, enabling full advantage to be taken of the wrap-round screen to increase the total angle of vision. Distortion at the curved ends was sufficiently slight not to be noticed. With a low scuttle and prominent helmet-shaped front wings, there is no difficulty in judging width and placing the car accurately, even for a driver of small stature. Rear wing extremities, too, are visible through the very large rear window, making reversing simple. An excellent view rearwards is provided by the mirror.

There is a sufficient range of adjustment of the one-piece front seat to enable tall or short drivers to find a good

A push-button catch releases the counter-balanced lid of the large boot. Some space is occupied by the spare wheel, but it should not be necessary to disturb luggage to reach it for a wheel change

driving position. Also, the seat runners are mounted on ramps, so that as the seat is brought forward it is raised to improve visibility for drivers of below-average height; at the same time this raises the knees rather high in relation to the pedals. The wheel is well placed for visibility over it. For drivers who like support for their arms, the centre folding armrest and the one on the door are placed correctly for this purpose.

As the test car was equipped with a manual gearbox (and optional Borg-Warner overdrive) it was possible to renew acquaintance with the very good example of steering column gear change which is fitted on the Zephyr. This is light and positive in its action, and all three gear positions are found readily. Synchromesh, provided on second and top gears, is seldom beaten, even in rapid movement of the lever during either upward or downward changes. Perhaps the most outstanding quality of this gearbox is the quietness of its indirect ratios, both being virtually inaudible. The only transmission noise detected at any time was a subdued whine when overdrive was engaged.

Getting away smoothly from rest required a little practice. This resulted from use of a linkage which gave rather rapid throttle opening during the initial movement of the accelerator. Combined with a fairly long though light clutch movement, this made judgment difficult. In heavy traffic, smooth crawling was not easy. Pedal angles of clutch and brake are not well chosen, so that the foot tends to slide across the pad.

Starting was certain with either a hot or cold engine; it is possible to lock the pull-out choke control in any position

by rotating the knob—a good feature. Six cylinders giving a swept volume of 2,553 c.c. endow the Zephyr with a very lively performance, though it goes about its task quietly and smoothly. When accelerating hard, a certain amount of exhaust noise can be heard from within the car, but the sound is not unpleasant. The engine is very flexible, but smoothness was marred at one point by carburettor hesitancy when pulling away from low speeds in top. With overdrive engaged some engine vibration is transmitted to the body below 32 m.p.h. in top gear.

For quite a large six-seater family car performance is sufficiently high to satisfy most people. Maximum speeds, limited by valve bounce, in first and second gears are 34 and 59 m.p.h. respectively. Second gear gives a fine surge of power for overtaking and there is little point in hanging on to it above about 50 m.p.h. before changing into top or overdrive second. High top-gear performance enables a driver to retain this ratio for long periods.

With overdrive engaged in second gear the maximum speed is 82 m.p.h. Overdrive can be obtained in first also, though to reach the minimum operating speed of 32 m.p.h. an engine speed very close to valve-bounce point is reached and it is not practical to use it regularly. With the Borg-Warner unit there is no safeguard against unintentional engagement of direct drive while travelling fast in overdrive second, so that at speeds above 59 m.p.h. operation of the kick-down switch would cause overrevving of the engine.

Chief advantage of the Borg-Warner overdrive is the reduction in engine speed for cruising. As is now well known, engagement is obtained, after first placing the facia control in overdrive position, by releasing the accelerator sufficiently to allow overrun to occur, in any gear, at any speed above 32 m.p.h. It is not a rapid change—if one hurries it may fail to engage. The car in overdrive top will cruise at speeds up to 75 m.p.h. in an effortless fashion and without signs of fussiness from the engine, which is turning over 30 per cent slower than in direct drive. Maximum speed obtainable in overdrive top is fractionally lower than in direct.

Re-engagement of direct drive is by a kick-down switch beneath the accelerator pedal and operated by moving the pedal beyond full-throttle position. The change takes place quite smoothly and direct drive is retained irrespective of the throttle position until overrun again occurs. A disadvantage of this arrangement is that overdrive will engage as soon as the driver lifts his foot to brake for a corner, during the time he might have preferred to remain in a lower gear. It is a simple matter for a switch to be added to the electrical circuit of the overdrive, to enable direct drive to be engaged without employing full throttle.

With overdrive selected, free-wheeling takes place below 27 m.p.h. in any gear, this being the fall-out speed. This release of engine braking can be detected, but it is not in the least disconcerting as it happens at low speed. After starting from rest, if second and top gears are selected below 32 m.p.h., clutchless changes can be made—and downshifts, too, of course—due to the freewheel action. Except for moving away and coming to rest, when the clutch has to be used, it is, therefore, possible to drive without touching the clutch pedal, although acceleration suffers with such early upward changes.

The overdrive unit was not designed with this practice in mind—it is purely incidental. A more worthwhile advantage is that is does enable first gear, which has no synchromesh, to be engaged easily and quietly, once the car is on the move. This can be done even without operating the clutch, if a suitable pause is made for syn-

The vacuum servo unit for the brakes can be seen on the right of the battery, the reservoir—used also for the vacuum-operated screen wipers—being mounted on the far side of the engine compartment

chronism before attempting the change. It is not easy to make a smooth take-up of the drive following freewheeling.

In the course of the 1,050 miles covered during the test an overall fuel consumption of 23·7 m.p.g. was recorded. There was much hard driving during this period, but full use was made of overdrive. In more leisurely motoring and limiting the speed to 50-55 m.p.h., 28 m.p.g. could be obtained easily. In heavy traffic, consumption rose to 22 m.p.g. These are good figures for a large car capable of quite high performance, and demonstrate the merits of high gearing and a high power-to-weight ratio, the kerb weight, which includes five gallons of fuel, being only 24cwt.

Premium fuel was used, and no pinking was noticed at any time. The effect which overdrive has on fuel consumption is shown by the figures quoted for sustained speeds. For example, at a steady 60 m.p.h. the consumption is improved from 24·7 to 30 m.p.g. with overdrive in use. With a capacity of 10·5 gallons, the fuel tank has a useful range of about 225 miles between refills. There is no reserve supply.

All who drove the car had unreserved praise for the brakes. Although disc brakes are fitted at the front only, the whole system is linked to a vacuum servo, and pedal effort is comparable with that of previous Zephyrs. This has

Wide opening doors and a not-too-low roof make entering the car an easy matter. Each seat will accommodate three in comfort, and there is sufficient leg room at the rear when the front seat has been set fully back

*There is excellent visibility
all round and the high,
clearly defined wing ex-
tremities assist the driver
when parking and reversing*

not been brought to the pitch where it becomes over sensitive, and at no time was there any tendency to overbrake.
The action is very smooth and progressive, and when applied
hard at high speeds the brakes slowed the car squarely, there
being no tendency for it to wander. A maximum pedal
effort of 75lb was required to give the best stopping figure
of 0·86g, at which the rear wheels locked first.

As is usually the case with disc brakes, their effectiveness
was slightly reduced during the first application or two
before they became warmed. This is noticed only after
driving away in the morning or after a spell of motorway
driving. Heavy rain did not affect their efficiency, and
squeal was noticed only on occasions during light application at low speeds. A large vacuum reservoir under the
bonnet ensures that assisted braking is available even with
a dead engine, and six successive applications were made
without losing vacuum.

Easily reached and applied, the pull-out handbrake lever
would only just hold the car, one up, on a 1-in-4 gradient.
The Zephyr restarted readily on this gradient but not on a
severe 1-in-3 slope, when clutch slip developed. Maximum
retardation, using the handbrake alone, was 0·22g from
30 m.p.h.

Generally, the standard of ride comfort of both front and
rear seats is high, and the suspension is capable of absorbing
bad surface irregularities without pitching. There is a feeling of great rigidity in the body, but on certain types of
poor surface tremors are transmitted directly through the
seat to the front passengers. The Zephyr is remarkably
free from road noise, and there is no roar over coarse
surfaces.

Seats are deeply upholstered, the squab of the front
one being very resilient. Lack of lateral location is noticed
during fast cornering.

Although its self-centring is strong, the steering is never
heavy even when parking. It is fairly low geared, but precise, and very little reaction is felt at the wheel. The chosen
line is held easily on a corner, little roll develops, even in
hard driving, and tyre squeal is evident only on smoother
types of surfaces. The Zephyr has quite strong understeer
and is very stable and predictable when cornered fast. It
runs straight and true with little conscious effort on the part
of the driver. Adhesion on a dry road is excellent. In the
wet, over-enterprising cornering can give rise to a lightening
of steering effort and the need for applying a larger-than-
usual steering lock; opening the throttle judiciously and
urging the car's tail round restores the stability. In
cornering the car felt more stable with the engine driving
it than on the overrun. It continued to handle well with
three passengers and a boot full of luggage.

Although the Zephyr was reluctant to spin its rear wheels
on a wet road when starting from rest, care sometimes had
to be taken to avoid opening the throttle too hurriedly when
accelerating away from a corner. Wet conditions generally
call for a sensitive throttle foot.

Minor controls have been well grouped to avoid con-
fusion, ignition-and-starter switch and lamp switch being
operated by the right hand, and choke and wiper controls
by the left. The lamp switch is of pull-out type, the first
pull giving parking lamps and the second headlamps.
These give a beam adequate for the performance of the car,
with good nearside illumination and wide spread in the
dipped position. The dip switch is in a convenient position
beside the clutch pedal.

Instruments have subdued but effective back lighting,
controlled by a rheostat which is regulated by rotating the
knob of the lamp switch. Wipers clear a very large area
of the screen and their arcs overlap at the centre. Being
vacuum-operated, the blades move more slowly during
acceleration, but nevertheless always keep moving, giving a
very fast wipe when the throttle is closed. It was possible
to adjust the speed of operation, but the control was rather
stiff on the test car.

Both front doors may be locked externally, and from the
inside by a plunger on each sill. This is pushed down for
the locked position (previously the action was reversed) and
is now less likely to be moved by young children. Internal
handles cannot be moved when this lock is engaged. Rear
doors are locked in the more conventional fashion by an
extra movement of the handle. A fresh-air heater and
demister, an optional extra on the Zephyr, was fitted and
proved to give powerful heating in the mild conditions
during the test. The controls near the centre of the facia
are placed so that it is not possible to read the various posi-

*Instruments are well arranged in such a position that the driver's eyes
have to be dropped the minimum amount to read them. There is ample
stowage space in the locker at the left of the facia and on the lined shelf*

Ford Zephyr . . .

tions marked on the quadrant, and these have to be memorized. A shortcoming of this unit is that the booster fan can be operated only in the hot or cold positions of the control and not in intermediate positions.

Large sun visors of safety pattern are fitted, being well padded and having collapsible frames. A rather unattractive seat covering material had been chosen on this car submitted for test—a drab coloured embossed plastic with a pleated, non-slip surface. The floors at both front and rear are carpeted; the standard of finish, both of the interior and the outside of the car, was of a high order, particularly so when related to the moderate price.

A new model push-button radio was fitted which gave good reception and could be tuned without moving the eyes from the road. Installed in the centre of the facia, it required a long reach of the driver.

The Zephyr continues to offer outstanding value for money. It is soundly engineered, has generous passenger and luggage space without being too large or unwieldy, performance in all aspects is excellent, and finish and refinement of running set a high standard in its class.

FORD ZEPHYR

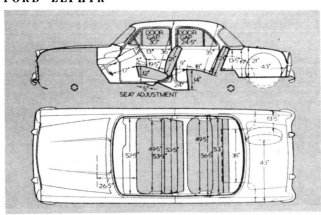

Scale ⅛in to 1ft. Driving seat in central position. Cushions uncompressed.

DATA

PRICE (basic), with saloon body, £610.
British purchase tax, £225 5s 10d.
Total (in Great Britain), £865 5s 10d.
Extras (Including P.T.): Radio £30 9s.
Heater £15 11s 8d. Overdrive £60 4s 2d.
Disc brakes £29 15s.

ENGINE: Capacity, 2,553 c.c. (155·8 cu in).
Number of Cylinders, 6.
Bore and stroke, 82·55 × 79·5 mm (3·25 × 3·12in).
Valve gear, overhead, pushrods.
Compression ratio, 7·8 to 1.
B.h.p. 85 (net) at 4,400 r.p.m. (b.h.p. per ton laden 62·7).
Torque, 133 lb ft at 2,000 r.p.m.
M.p.h. per 1,000 r.p.m. in top gear, 18·5.
M.p.h. per 1,000 r.p.m. in overdrive, 26·4.

WEIGHT: (With 5 gals fuel), 24 cwt (2,705 lb).
Weight distribution (per cent): F, 57; R, 43.
Laden as tested, 27 cwt (3,041lb).
Lb per c.c. (laden), 1·19.

BRAKES: Type, Girling, discs front, L and T drum brakes rear.
Method of operation, hydraulic, vacuum servo.
Disc diameter, F, 9·75in.
Drum dimensions, R, 9in diameter; 1·75in wide.
Swept area: 299 sq. in. total (262 sq. in. per ton laden).

TYRES: 6·40–13in Goodyear All Weather.
Pressures (p.s.i.); F, 24; R, 24 (normal).

TANK CAPACITY: 10·5 Imperial gallons.
Oil sump, 7 pints.
Cooling system, 22 pints (plus 1 pint if heater fitted).

DIMENSIONS: Wheelbase, 8ft 11in.
Track: F, 4ft 5in; R, 4ft 4in.
Length (overall), 14ft 11·04in.
Width, 5ft 8·87in.
Height, 5ft 0·62in.
Ground clearance, 6·8in.
Frontal area, 22·2 sq ft (approximately).
Luggage space, 18 cu ft (approximately).

ELECTRICAL SYSTEM: 12-volt; 57 ampère-hour battery.
Headlamps: 45-40 watt bulbs.

SUSPENSION: Front, independent, coil springs, anti-roll bar.
Rear, live axle, half-elliptic leaf springs.

PERFORMANCE

ACCELERATION TIMES (mean):
Speed range, Gear Ratios and Time in Sec.

m.p.h.	*2·73 to 1	3·90 to 1	*4·49 to 1	6·40 to 1	*7·76 to 1	11·08 to 1
10—30	—	8·8	—	5·3	—	3·7
20—40	—	8·9	—	5·3	—	5·7
30—50	15·8	9·1	8·6	5·7	—	—
40—60	19·0	11·0	10·5	—	—	—
50—70	19·5	13·8	15·3	—	—	—

*Overdrive.

From rest through gears to:

30 m.p.h.	..	4·6sec
40 "	..	8·0 "
50 "	..	11·2 "
60 "	..	16·5 "
70 "	..	26·8 "
80 "	..	37·4 "

Standing quarter mile 20·9sec.

MAXIMUM SPEEDS ON GEARS:

Gear		m.p.h.	k.p.h.
O.D.	(best)	90·0	144·8
Top	(mean)	90·8	146·2
	(best)	91·0	146·4
O.D. 2nd	..	82	132·0
2nd	..	59	95·0
O.D. 1st	..	47	75·6
1st	..	34	54·7

TRACTIVE EFFORT (by Tapley meter):

			Pull (lb per ton)	Equivalent gradient
O.D. Top	..	..	175	1 in 12·7
Top	..	..	270	1 in 8·2
O.D. second	..	..	300	1 in 7·4
Second	..	..	460	1 in 4·8

SPEEDOMETER CORRECTION: M.P.H.

Car speedometer	10	20	30	40	50	60	70	80	90	100
True speed	8	17	26	36	45	54	64	73	82·5	90

BRAKES (at 30 m.p.h. in neutral):

Pedal load in lb	Retardation	Equiv. stopping distance in ft
25	0·23g	131
50	0·59g	51
75	0·87g	34·7

FUEL CONSUMPTION (at steady speeds in

		Direct Top	O.D. Top
30 m.p.h.		32·8 m.p.g.	38·9 m.p.g.
40 "		30·6 "	35·7 "
50 "		28·0 "	33·1 "
60 "		24·7 "	30·0 "
70 "		21·0 "	25·6 "
80 "		17·3 "	19·8 "

Overall fuel consumption for 1,050 miles, 23·7 m.p.g. (11·9 litres per 100 km.).
Approximate normal range 22-28 m.p.g. (12·8—10·1 litres per 100 km.).
Fuel: Premium grades.

TEST CONDITIONS: Weather: Wet, light breeze.
Air temperature, 60 deg. F.
Model described in *The Autocar* of 27 February 1959.

STEERING: Turning circle.
Between kerbs, R, 38ft 7in. L, 38ft 3in.
Between walls, R, 40ft 9in. L, 40ft 5in.
Turns of steering wheel from lock to lock, 3·5.

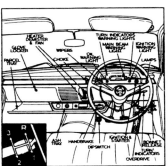

OWNER'S VIEW

Michael Allen talks to Stuart Clarke, who, some five years ago, at the tender age of sixteen, bought himself a Mk1 Consul on which to learn to drive, and to serve as a stepping-stone to owning his "dream car" – a Mk2. That ambition became a reality a year or so ago when Stuart purchased a 1957 Consul.

M.A. Why is it that you are so attracted to the big Mk2 Fords?

S.C. Originally it was the American influence. When I was a very small boy in the 1960s I preferred the fifties American styles, and to me the Mk2s were the nearest British equivalent – a beautiful looking object.

M.A. When did you buy your Mk2?

S.C. Well, as you know, I started with a Mk1 – another of my favourites – but I decided to start looking for an early Mk2 with that now quite rare, very transatlantic interior, a year or so ago.

M.A. What condition was it in?

S.C. Completely solid underneath, but rather tatty-looking on the body. It did have rust in some of the usual Mk2 places, the rear wheel arches etc., and as it had been stored for 14 years the paintwork was badly oxidised.

M.A. What renovation work have you carried out?

S.C. I fitted a new nearside front wing and door myself, but had the rear wheel arches professionally repaired as the shape is quite subtle. This turned out to be the right move, I'm well pleased with the job. I repainted the whole front end, and of course faded-in the rear arches. A lot of T-cut brought the rest of the paintwork up quite well. I've filled the sills with old engine oil, and cleaned and Waxoyled the entire undersides.

M.A. Bearing these jobs in mind, would it perhaps have been more economical to have bought a car in better condition than yours initially?

S.C. Well, yes if I would have been quite happy with a Low-Line Consul, of which there are more available, but as I really wanted one of the earlier cars which are now comparatively rare, I had less of a choice.

M.A. Have you had problems obtaining spare parts at all?

S.C. No. It never ceases to amaze me just how much there is still about for these cars. Of course, it pays to have plenty of contacts in the old-car scene. I soon located scrapped early Mk2s which provided some useful spares, and for service items I've found that the motor factors can still get most things quickly if they haven't already got them in stock. Then there are the specialists, too.

M.A. Do you find the performance sufficient today?

S.C. It's good enough, but by 1.7 litre standards now its obviously not a fast car. It cruises really well in the sixties, though.

M.A. And the handling?

S.C. Actually, it was on radials, but I didn't like the feel somehow. It corners well on cross-plies, and is now very predictable.

M.A. Do you use the Consul on a regular basis?

S.C. Oh yes, I think of it in that respect as it was originally intended – to be used.

M.A. How practical do you find it, and have you found the running cost to be high?

S.C. It's very practical, no bother at all in modern traffic. I like the column gearchange better than any floor change I've ever driven. It has to be said that in many ways it's more practical than a modern car. If necessary, it will seat six comfortably, and they can get in and out easily; yes, as a passenger car, it's very practical indeed. Overall, the running costs are quite low, as although it has to be said that it's a bit thirsty by today's 1.7 litre standards, spares are extremely cheap by comparison. Also of course it was designed by engineers who gave serious thought to ease of servicing and maintenance, and that keeps costs down too.

M.A. Has your car won any prizes in concours events?

S.C. No. It's now looking quite tidy, but it's not in the prizewinning category. I do enter many shows though, its always worth going for the enjoyment of just being in touch with other enthusiasts.

M.A. How about the owners' club meetings?

S.C. I get to most of the Yorkshire meetings which are held jointly with the Mk1 club, of which I'm still also a member incidentally, and so know most of the Mk2 owners around here.

M.A. How would you sum up the enjoyment you derive from owning a Mk2 Consul?

S.C. Immeasurable. I have no intention of ever being without a Mk2, it just suits me in everything it does.

M.A. So, what advice then would you give to a potential owner?

S.C. Ideally, talk to someone who had a good example, and if possible examine theirs to establish what a good one should be like. Then, if you've got the money, go ahead and buy one.

Michael Allen interviews Steve Pickles, owner of a 1960 Zephyr for the past year after a succession of more modern small to medium sized models.

M.A. Just why are you so interested in the Ford Mk2 range?

S.P. I've been in love with them ever since being a small child. Although my father always had a car, the first trip to leave any lasting impression was in a friend's father's blue Consul.

M.A. When did you eventually buy your own Mk2?

S.P. Well, I was very disappointed at just missing a slightly damaged Consul about 1973/74, it actually went for scrap. As there wasn't any really organised old-car scene then anyway, I just purchased a second-hand small car, and followed this with other used, supposedly economical models. I didn't even know a Mk2 club had come into existence, and then I saw your first book "Consul Zephyr Zodiac" advertised, and after reading it I just had to get into the Mk2 scene. I bought the Zephyr through an ad. in one of the advertising weeklies.

M.A. What sort of condition was it in?

S.P. The bodywork was fine, amazingly rot-free, but with some evidence of partial respraying in recent years. Mechanically, however, there was one serious problem, as the engine had a misfire which was due to a couple of burned-out exhaust valves. In other respects the mechanical condition was really good.

M.A. What then, have the repairs etc. been so far?

S.P. Well, the engine of course had to be attended to right-away. As there was a service history with the car which confirmed the mileometer reading of 90,000 to be correct, and also that no work had ever been done to the engine it seemed wise to have an extensive overhaul as the cylinder head had to come off to attend to

the valves. The bore wear was surprisingly small, and so new pistons with a stepped top ring and a lower oil control ring around the skirt were fitted without the need to remove the block from the car. New standard size bearing shells were fitted, and the top-end work consisted of a decoke, new exhaust valves and new valve springs. Since then, the only big replacement has been a new exhaust system. Apart from a steam-clean and thorough Waxoyling underneath, I've not spent anything yet on the bodywork.

M.A. Taking into account the engine overhaul, would it have been more economical to have looked out for a better car in this respect?

S.P. Possibly, but it's hard to say really, as the car was very attractively priced. In fact, the purchase price, plus the cost of engine parts and labour, came to almost exactly a quarter of the cost of a new basic BL Metro, and I don't think you can expect to buy a very good all round Zephyr for much less. much less.

M.A. Was there any difficulty in obtaining the parts you needed?

S.P. No, although they did come from two different sources. The decoke set from Ford 50 Spares, and the pistons etc. from the Newford Parts Centre. The exhaust system which I bought recently came from Goldendays Motor Services.

I'm very pleased with the spares situation, and particularly the prices which are a lot better than for my previous car which was an Eastern European product.

M.A. Having got the engine into a healthy condition, how do you rate the performance?

S.P. It's a very quick motor, it surprises many people in modern cars when it overtakes them, particularly on hills.

M.A. Does the handling match the acceleration available?

S.P. Oh yes, although I must admit that I was unsure of the steering at first, mainly because it's so much lighter than anything else I'd ever driven. But having got used to it I'm still surprised at just how well this model goes round corners, you can certainly drive it hard with complete confidence.

M.A. I believe you use the car for going to work most days in addition to weekend trips etc., do you find it practical for this type of constant use?

S.P. Very practical, more practical in fact than any car I've ever owned previously. It's so roomy that it takes everything a family needs when going on holiday, it's more comfortable than the cramped low-built modern cars, and it really is easy to drive. You can see all four wing tips from the driving seat, and that makes parking a doddle. The same good visibility makes town driving easy, as does the fact that you're not going up and down through the gearbox all the time either, the torque from very low speeds in top is amazing. On the open road it spends most of its time in overdrive, with the occasional kick-down into direct top for the steeper hills or some quick overtaking.

M.A. Do you regard it as an economical car?

S.P. Very definitely, there's no depreciation on a car like this if you've bought it at the right price for the model and then keep it in at least the same condition. Spares prices are much cheaper than for modern cars in my experience, and even garage work can turn out cheaper because the Mk2 is so easy to work on. All this more than offsets the petrol consumption which is probably a bit heavier than on a modern $2^1/2$ litre "six", although mine doesn't drop as low as 20mpg on local work, and has managed just over 30mpg on trips to the coast. The overdrive helps of course.

M.A. You do seem impressed so far with the spares prices, has any particular spares specialist been especially helpful?

S.P. To be honest, I have no complaints with each of them tried so far, that is the Newford Parts Centre, Ford 50 Spares, and Goldendays Motor Services. With the three of them it does mean that if one hasn't got the part you want, one of the others may well have.

M.A. Has your car won any prizes in concours events?

S.P. No. It's a good clean and sound Mk2, but not in the concours class where the standards are now very high. I do got to events though, it's always a good day out whether you've a chance of winning something or not.

M.A. In their day, the Mk2 Zephyrs were successful racing and rallying saloons, and more recently have been seen in Classic events, have you thought of ever participating with your Zephyr?

S.P. Oh no, it is the family car. In fact, as it is painted in Imperial maroon my wife has named it "Duchess", and even refers to it as that rather than the Zephyr. I don't think she would approve of it being raced.

M.A. How helpful have you found it to belong to the owners' club?

S.P. Well the club also does some spare parts, so it is yet another source, although I haven't needed anything from them as yet. I enjoy the regular newsletter which often contains useful tips etc., and I get to some of the northern meetings.

M.A. How would you sum up the enjoyment you get from your Zephyr?

S.P. Well, in many respects really, being a well-styled, very good-looking car, I get enjoyment out of simply looking at it. I enjoy driving it for its own sake, and also just being involved with other club members and old-car enthusiasts in general.

M.A. What advice would you give to potential owners of the Mk2 Zephyr?

S.P. Buy one, they are well worth it from the sheer enjoyment you can have with them. If you can't afford a separate collectors' car, then sell your modern car and get a Zephyr for everyday use, thats the best advice I can give.

BUYING

Which model?

Fortunately, sufficient numbers of all three basic variations of the Mk2 model have survived, so a distinct choice of Consul, Zephyr or Zodiac can be made in the knowledge that examples for sale somewhere in the country can be found at almost any given time. If, however, a specific variation of one of the basic themes is wanted, then things can become difficult, as the large majority of surviving Mk2s are the post-February 1959 Low-Line saloon models, and even on these the overdrive, and particularly the automatic transmission option are rare. So, if the choice is, for exmple, simply a Low-Line Consul saloon, then things should not prove very difficult, whereas the desire for a 1957 Zephyr, with the early grille and automatic transmission, could cause considerable frustration; this comment applying also of course to the extremely rare estate car or convertible models, a suitable example of either of which could literally take years to find. Therefore, if the standard transmission is considered to be perfectly adequate, which it most certainly was to the majority of

buyers of these cars, and always bearing in mind that essentially the Zephyr and Zodiac are virtually the same car, it is better to decide which model on the basis of whether a four- or six-cylinder engine is required.

Although four-cylinder cars, which share similar bodywork with a six-cylinder stablemate, are often thought of as being underpowered, this particular criticism of the Consul from some quarters was not really justified. Compared with its four-cylinder rivals the Consul in fact offered rather more in both speed and acceleration, and whilst in no way ever being a "performance car" as such, it is still quite capable of sensible cross-country averages over give-and-take roads, under which conditions second gear can be used profitably up to 50mph or so for overtaking purposes should the Consul have been baulked to unreasonably low speeds. On the motorway, a 70mph cruising speed is equivalent to 4,150rpm, at which rate a healthy Consul engine will not complain. It will, however, consume petrol at the rate of 20 to 21mpg at this speed, and if a Consul is being chosen primarily for its 30mpg touring fuel consumption potential, then cruising speeds in the order of 50 to 55mph will have to be accepted. For those willing to accept these limitations, and who perhaps have no desire for the superior acceleration and increased engine smoothness of the six-cylinder cars, then the Consul can indeed be a very attractive proposition, offering useful further economies over the Zephyr and Zodiac due to normally being priced somewhat lower than the apparently more glamorous "sixes", whilst attracting appreciably lower insurance premiums by virtue of its smaller engine.

Offering the same accommodation, but appreciably more performance throughout the entire speed range, the Zephyrs

and Zodiacs are very much at home in today's conditions in which their flexible six-cylinder engines provide really useful performance right where it is needed most. To put the performance into perspective it is only necessary to quote 30 – 50mph times of around $8\frac{1}{2}$ and 6 seconds in top and second gear, respectively, these figures being better than some of today's very genuine 100mph cars. In fact, it is only above 80mph or so that the Mk2 Zephyr begins to lose out to much of the modern competition. The excellent top gear performance from very low speeds aids the fuel consumption figures considerably, and bearing this in mind the Zephyr should not necessarily be dismissed on economic grounds, as there is no need to always be using all the performance available. The optional overdrive is worth some 5 or 6mpg extra on a long-distance journey, but, unfortunately, this equipment is comparatively rare, as these cars are reasonably high-geared anyway, and were introduced at a time when much of the main-road network in Britain was single carriageway with no opportunities for sustained high-speed cruising, and the motorway system was still several years away. If a considerable amount of motorway driving is inevitable, and at speeds in the vicinity of the legal limit, then the six-cylinder models are the obvious choice, as at anything between 70 to 80mph (the Consul's maximum) they use less fuel than the four-cylinder model whilst running in an altogether more effortless manner.

Examination

The relatively straight-forward nature of the Mk2 Fords makes it comparitively easy to assess the condition of one of these being examined with a view to purchase, and with generally good mechanical spares availability today from several sources it is not necessary to dismiss a Mk2 purely on the grounds of poor mechanical condition, always assuming of course that the price does reflect that state of affairs. When checking out the engine it must be remembered that excessive blue smoke in the exhaust on these cars can be caused by the failure of the diaphragm in the vacuum pump, which then allows oil to be pumped into the inlet manifold, actually causing oiling up of the plugs in some instances. If this is the case, an exchange fuel/vacuum pump, or alternatively a vacuum pump overhaul kit is required. When re-starting a hot engine some blue smoke may be evident once again, due this time to oil escaping past the valve stem oil seals which have a tendency to become hard with age. This can usually be ignored, as oil seepage here is actually only slight, and has little effect on the overall oil consumption.

Apart from these instances the Mk2 engines burn very little oil if in good condition, generally less in fact on today's multigrade oils than was the case in their heyday on the straight 20-grade lubricants recommended, so little blue smoke should be evident if the bores, pistons and rings are in good condition. The ventilation system of these units results in some fumes and oil-mist being visible from the rocker cover breather/oil filler cap, and also from the crankcase breather tube; this quickly results in a rather dirty engine externally, but has the real benefit of keeping the unit very clean inside. Even under cold, short distance stop and start running these engines rarely suffer from the internal sludging which afflicts so many others. If everything is in good order, the most noticeable noise will come from the valve gear, which, even

with the rockers adjusted correctly, always seems to be audible on these engines. Both the gearbox and final drive should be quiet on the move; a slight "moan" from the rear axle is acceptable, but should not be obtrusive. If the gearbox is in good order the synchromesh should be almost unbeatable; on high-mileage cars second gear may jump out of engagement sometimes on the overrun, but this doesn't usually lead to any further trouble, and some owners drive a Mk2 in this condition for years. The exposed gearchange mechanism of the early cars, and that of the Low-Line models should be very positive, and quick; whilst the concentric gearchange of the 1958 models is somehow lacking in feel by comparison, although by overall column-change standards it is quite reasonable.

Those who have never sampled a Burman steering box may well have difficulty in assessing the condition of the steering gear when first driving a Mk2, particularly on the post-October 1957 models with the recirculating ball mechanism. Above 20 to 25mph, when running on the model's correct cross-ply tyres, there is virtually no feel at the steering wheel. This can give rise to an impression of vagueness which is amplified somewhat by the fact that the very wide, and rather flat bonnet is devoid of an aiming point, thus making the Mk2 seem a little difficult to place accurately. In fact, growing familiarity soon brings complete confidence, even to the point of making other steering arrangements seem unnecessarily heavy. With the car stationary, check the actual free-play at the steering wheel rim where there should be little more than half an inch play if the steering gear is in good condition. Although the track rod ends, track control arms etc., will almost certainly have been renewed, the original steering box may well still

be on the car as these boxes are adjustable for wear and of a high quality, generally lasting extremely well. The suspension units too, were long-life components, with the benefit of level/filler plugs to allow topping up with fluid when seepage eventually occurs. Whilst the front coil springs last well, the rear leaf springs tend to flatten out after an extensive mileage, and a broken leaf or two may be found on a Mk2 which is sitting a bit low at the back. The braking system on these cars can seize up after only very short periods of inactivity, and this should be remembered when inspecting a car which has seen only infrequent use or has been laid up for some time immediately prior to being offered for sale.

With several good spares sources, including the owners' club, a Mk2 can be kept in good running order with no more inconvenience than most present-day cars, and in fact with appreciably less trouble than some. Therefore, always assuming that the price of the car under consideration takes into account any mechanical defects, a Mk2 need not be rejected on mechanical grounds.

The integrally constructed bodyshell has excellent rigidity when in good condition, relying on the inner sills for some of that rigidity in the lower regions, and serious corrosion in the inner sills is a legitimate MOT failure point in so far as the bodyshell is concerned, and particularly so if the rot has spread to the inner membrane running inside the box section. Fortunately, unlike many other cars with MacPherson strut front suspension, including some later Fords, the Mk2 rarely suffers from corrosion at the suspension top mounting. This is because the mounting point in the inner wing is shaped to embrace the upper part of the strut, so shielding the mounting area quite effectively from much of the road dirt thrown up. Nevertheless, a check should still be made here, as there have been cases where rust has taken a hold at this point. The front wings rust visibly around the headlight area, and again from top to bottom along their rear edge. Being bolted on, however, makes the front wings relatively easy to remove for repair or replacement, but at the rear the situation is somewhat difficult as the wings here are a welded up part of the integral construction. Aft of the rear wheel arch, a lower inner wing projects downwards from the boot floor to meet the lower edge of the outer wing. This forms a well, and although a drain hole was provided in manufacture this often silts up with the result that many Mk2s eventually suffer from rotted-out rear wing bottoms; this state of affairs however is not particularly serious from a structural point of view, as the join along here plays only a very small part in the overall rigidity.

With an estate car, apart from the need to take into account the condition of the tailgate, for which replacements are virtually unobtainable apart from the window which is the Mk1 Consul/Zephyr item, the previous comments regarding the saloons apply, but the also rare convertible model does pose some difficult problems. On the road, over poorly maintained surfaces, there will be some evidence of scuttle shake even in a good example, with perhaps more creaks and rattles making themselves heard than would be the case with the average Mk2 saloon. To keep these effects minimal, good underbody condition is vital, as despite the additional reinforcing welded in during manufacture the floorpan is still under rather more strain than that of the saloon. First class examples rarely change hands, and anyone seeking a convertible will almost certainly be faced with some restoration work, and another point worth noting is that spares for the power hood mechanism, if needed, could be

difficult to find.

Recently, repair sections for some of the model's vulnerable areas, such as around the headlamps, and the rear wheel arch lip, have become available, and the Mk2 club is looking further into the possibility of other repair panels to ease the situation regarding bodywork restoration.

Historical Value Patterns

During their production run, the second-hand values of the Mk2 range remained reasonably high with the Consuls, due to their potential economy, generally suffering rather less depreciation that the two six-cylinder cars. During the mid/late 1960s economic boom, by which time the Mk2 was an obsolete model anyway, prices fell dramatically almost irrespective of condition at a time when the "newness" of a car became quite a status symbol even if the model in question was right at the bottom of the used car market.

In recent years the surviving Mk2s have grown steadily in value, with the performance potential of the six-cylinder models now appearing to outweigh the economy of the Consul with the result that, in any given condition, one of the six-cylinder cars will usually change hands for appreciably more money than if it was a "four". Being relatively plentiful has, however, kept Mk2 saloon prices at a sensible level within the collectors' car scene, and even the scarcity of the Farnham estate car does not seem to have set its value any higher. With the convertibles, however, things are

different; these are regarded by many people as the most "collectible" of the Mk2 range, and, in Zephyr/Zodiac configuration they are also attractive to those who otherwise have no particular interest in a Ford but who wish for a powerful drophead car. This has resulted in convertible prices usually reflecting the scarcity of the model rather than the particular car's condition, with first class examples seemingly proving to be worth around twice the price of an equivalent saloon.

Summing Up

A Mk2 can be a thoroughly practical proposition today, and in fact is usually appreciably better value than the similarly priced modern cars which are nearing the bottom of the normal used car market.

Whilst some searching will almost certainly be necessary, it should not take too long for someone willing to travel in order to view, to find a sound, and sensibly priced saloon. The advertisements in the "classic" motoring monthlies are a good place to find there cars on offer, and the enthusiast who is committed to acquiring a Mk2 would be advised to join the owners' club before a purchase has been made, as there are usually a small number for sale amongst the club membership at any given time.

CLUBS, SPECIALISTS & BOOKS

Clubs

A Mk2 owners' club was formed in Britain in 1977, and has since grown to more than 800 members. The services offered to its members by this well-organised club are a bi-monthly newsletter containing features, advice, members letters, sales & wants etc: a wide range of spare parts, including some remanufactured bodywork items: several major meetings each year at venues chosen to appeal to a wide section of the membership, local meetings, and club participation in "open" events.

Several clubs catering for these models are well-established in Australia and New Zealand, being organised on a more local basis owing to the greater distances between townships. Owing to the relatively smaller number of these cars "down under", the clubs there encompass all models, Marks 1 to 4, of the Consul Zephry Zodiac series.

Ford Mk2 Consul Zephyr Zodiac Owners' Club. Dave Debenham, 170 Conisborough Crescent, Catford, London SE6

Consul Zephyr Zodiac Club (Wellington Inc). Bob Crozier, PO Box 1585, Wellington, New Zealand.

Auckland Consul Zephyr Zodiac Car Club. Graeme Parsons, PO Box 30179, Takapuna North, New Zealand.

The Zodiac & Zephyr Club (Southland) inc. 5 Nevis Crescent, Invercargill, New Zealand.

Zephyr Zodiac Car Club (Christchurch) Inc. Mrs Maureen Anthony, PO Box 21157, Christchurch, New Zealand.

Zephyr Zodiac Club of Otago Peter Matheson, 16 Eglinton Road, Dunedin, New Zealand.

Nelson Zephyr Zodiac Club Tim Readley, 10 Colman Street, Richmond, Nelson, New Zealand.

Classic Zephyr Zodiac Enthusiasts Club Greg Price, c/o The Post Office, Paremoremo, Auckland, New Zealand.

Zephyr Zodiac Club (Herewhenua) John Clime, 10 Margret Street, Levin, New Zealand.

Zephyr Zodiac Owner's Club (Central Region) Bryan Brickley, PO Box 5128, Palmerston North, New Zealand.

Hamilton Zephyr Zodiac Club Mrs Rochelle Hooper, PO Box Box 4295, Hamilton East, New Zealand

Consul Zephyr Zodiac Club of New South Wales. John Bourke, 172 Ridge Road, Engadine, NSW Australia.

Zephyr & Zodiac Club of Melbourne. PO Box 86, Surrey Hills, Victoria, Australia.

Consul Zephyr Zodiac Car Club of Queensland. PO Box 279, Salisbury 4107, Queensland Australia.

Zephyr Zodiac Owners' Club of Western Australia Mrs Sue Roberts, 70a Glenelg Avenue, Wembly Downs, Western Australia.

Spares Specialists

Many routine service items for these cars can still be purchased from motor factors, but most spares will have to be obtained from the specialists dealing with the models concerned, particularly so in respect of reconditioned items, such as MacPherson struts etc., which will usually be available on an exchange basis.

Newford Parts Centre. Prop. J. Horridge, Abbey Mill, Abbey Village, Chorley, Lancashire, England.

Ford 50 Spares, Prop. K. Tingey, 69 Jolliffe Road, Poole, Dorset, BH15 2HA, England.

Goldendays Motor Services. Prop. J. Blythe, Boundary Garage, Cromer Road, Norwich, England.

Books

Several of the owner's handbook, and the rather more comprehensive workshop type manuals were available during the late 1950s and 1960s for these models. All of these bar one, are however now out-of-print, but do appear occasionally amongst the stock of specialists motoring book shops. Additionally, the Ford Motor Company's own workshop repair manuals and spare parts manuals were distributed exclusively throughout the Ford dealership network for their use only. Copies of these extremely useful books however, have found their way on to the shelves of second-hand car book shops in recent years, and are well worth purchasing when found.

Still in print and available from motoring bookshops: Ford Consul Zephyr and Zodiac; Owner's Workshop Manual. Published by the Haynes

Publishing Group, this manual deals comprehensively with all major repair procedures on the Mk1, Mk2, and M3 range of models.

From the historical point of view, nothing was published about these cars until my own major work on the subject: Consul Zephyr Zodiac; The Big Fifties

Fords, which appeared in November 1983. This is an in-depth history of the preceding Mk1 models and the Mk2 range, and includes the full competition history. Published by Motor

Racing Publications, it is still in print and available from motoring bookshops.

1

2

PHOTO GALLERY

4

3

5

1. The slender pillars allowed almost unobstructed all-round vision on the new Mk2 models. The hooded headlamps, and the mesh grille of the Consul gave just a hint of the American Ford Thunderbird sports coupe to this British family model Ford. The overriders were always an optional extra on the Consul.

2. The mildly finned rear wings could be seen from the driving seat through the panoramic rear window. The horizontal flutes in the back panel appeared in October 1965. The Webasto type sunroof was not a Ford listed option, but was a popular accessory during the 1950s.

3. Head and sidelamp detail. This Consul has been subsequently equipped with Lucas Hi-Power headlamps in place of the original units.

4. Quite discreet tail lamp treatment was an early-Consul feature, with the standard reflectors looking something of an afterthought.

5. Wheel and tyre detail. Tubeless cross-ply tyres were the standard specification on the Mk2 model. The original 5.90 x 13 size for the Consul is now hard to obtain, and this car is running on the very slightly larger 6.00 x 13 covers.

6. The slightly longer nose necessary to house the six-cylinder engine, and a completely different grille identify the Zephyr from the front. This early grille, which was replaced in October 1957, has become known by no less than three alternative names, being referred to by today's enthusiasts as the "honeycombe", "egg-crate", or, in Australia, the "chip cutter". At the rear, the upswept chromium side strips and longer fins were Zephyr identification features.

6

7

8

9

7. Unmistakable in its two-tone paintwork and other embellishments, the top-of-the-range Zodiac.

8. & 9. Unlike earlier Zodiacs, the Mk2 had its own special front and rear treatment. The fuel filler is behind the numberplate as on the two cheaper Mk2 models.

10. The "washboard" panel is in a silver-painted finish.

11. The rear pillar chrome trim appeared in October 1956.

12. The front wing badge was applied to all models on both sides.

13. If the optional overdrive, or the automatic transmission was fitted, this was proclaimed in suitable additional script on the boot lid.

14. A graceful, dished two-spoke steering wheel faced the driver, with the lack of a horn-ring here indicating a Consul, as both the Zephyr and Zodiac featured a hornring. The moulded rubber floorcovering of the Consul is also evident here. The instrument cluster and facia panel was the same in all three models. A lift-up ashtray is placed centrally.

10

11

12

13

14

15. The exposed gearchange linkage was a feature of the early Mk2 cars.

16. An ashtray for those in the rear was placed conveniently at the back of the front seat. Full width seating gave very ample three- abreast accommodation.

17. A wide underbonnet gave generally good accessibility, with the bulkhead-mounted hydraulic reservoirs, and the battery being easily reached on the offside. The heater unit is shaped to fit the bulkhead, with the air intake on the scuttle being well away from the exhaust fumes of other traffic ahead.

18. Estate cars became available in late 1956, and seen here are a Consul (left), Zephyr (centre), and a Zodiac at various stages of conversion in the workshops of the coachbuilders E.D. Abbott.

19. A small number of pick-up trucks were built at Dagenham, and this is thought to be one of those, although the Ford caption to this archive shot simply says "1957 Australian Pick-Up Zephyr".

20. The genuine Australian assembled pick-up featured a different rear cab structure from that shown in the previous illustration. The rear window is from the Mk1 saloon. All the Australian pick-ups featured Consul tail lamps, and this example is in fact a Zephyr which was photographed in 1981 – still hard at work.

21. & 22. These illustrations depict a 1957 Australian prototype Zephyr station wagon. Interesting points are the squared up rear passenger doors and the drop down tailgate with a rear window which was first wound down out-of-sight before lowering the tailgate. Cut-down overriders were necessary to allow the tailgate to open horizontally. Production of these in fact did not begin until 1959, by which time the Low Line

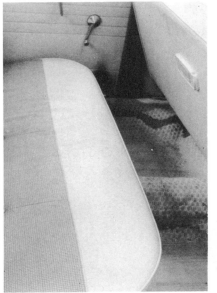

16

17

18

19

20

21

models had appeared. The rear view here depicts well the early Mk2 Zephyr tail lamp treatment.

23. Another interesting Australian variation, this time a Zephyr ambulance converted from a pick-up truck.

22

23

24

25

24. Even rarer! A Dagenham-built prototype of a proposed two-door pillarless coupe Zodiac. This car was powered by a triple Zenith carburettor engine based on the tuned units of the 1956 Alpine Rally Zephyrs, and would have been useful in that it would have homologated the triple carburettor set up for competition purposes and therefore allowed Zephyrs so equipped to compete as standard cars. In the event, lack of any spare production capacity was probably the reason why it never saw production.

25. A new grille, incorporating Zodiac-style sidelamps identified the Zephyr from October 1957 onwards.

26. The concentric gearchange mechanism of the 1958 model cars gave a neater look than the earlier exposed type, but unfortunately proved to be somewhat less accurate.

26

27. The redesigned rear pillar trim applied to all the 1958 model cars.

28. & 29. The Low-Line models had a rather sleeker appearance, and considerably more bright-metal trim. The two-tone paint, grille badge, and chrome cappings on the back panel flutes identify this as a De Luxe Consul. The lack of the triangular wing badges in this case is due to wing replacement at some stage. Like many Mk2s JSV 302 has acquired a set of later hubcaps and Mk3 Zodiac wheeltrims.

30. Although acquiring the Zephyr-type pointed wing tips, the Low-Line Consul retained the earlier Consul bumper which was now on extended mounting brackets, thus protecting the longer tips, and increasing the car's overall length very slightly.

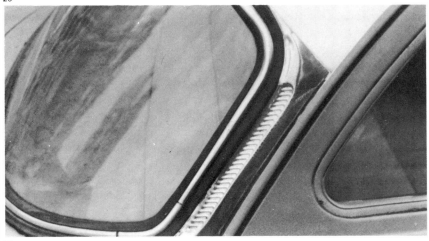

27

28

29

30

31

32

33

34

31. & 32. The Low-Line Zephyr, with the lack of rear wing script denoting a post-May 1961 car complete with disc brakes and sealed-beam headlamps. Zodiac wheeltrims have been fitted in this case.

33. & 34. A late model Low-Line Zodiac with the 109E Classic wheeltrims which were adopted by the Mk2 Zodiac during its last few months of production. The triangular wing badge was deleted from very late production Mk2s and in some cases replaced by a low-mounted traditional Ford oval badge on one side only.

35. The Low-Line instrument panel and facia. The half horn-ring was so as not to obscure the view of the instruments. The T handle visible above the wheel spoke is the overdrive manual lock-out control. The pull-out ashtray is in the bright-trim panel beneath the wheel spoke. The "blind" hole alongside is for the optional cigar lighter if fitted to the two cheaper cars.

36. & 37. General interior views of the Low-Line Zephyr. The front seat armrest was a standard feature of the six-cylinder models and the Consul De Luxe, with rear seat armrests being optional equipment. The headlining was a light-coloured vinyl on all models, and only the basic Consul came with a plain steering wheel and centre horn-button, and a rubber floorcovering.

35

36

37

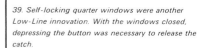

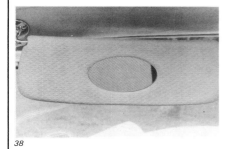

38

39

38. Crushable sunvisors were Low-Line features, that depicted here being the Zodiac type with a passenger's vanity mirror.

39. Self-locking quarter windows were another Low-Line innovation. With the windows closed, depressing the button was necessary to release the catch.

40. All the Low-Line cars featured a chromed headlamp hood with a less sharp profile than the previous painted type.

41. The new front and rear screen surrounds were in a rustless chromium alloy and were the same for all three cars. The chrome door window surround previously found only on Zephyrs and Zodiacs was now applied to the Consul.

42. This anodized aluminium wheeltrim was standard equipment on the Low-Line Zodiac and Consul De Luxe, replacing the previous chromed ring which was a Zodiac-only feature on the earlier cars.

43. Appropriate script on the Consul's boot lid accompanied the De Luxe specification. The redesigned Consul tail lamp treatment is well depicted here.

44. The Low-Line Zephyr tail lamp ...

45. ... and that of the Low-Line Zodiac. The sickle-shaped rear bumper was common to both six-cylinder cars, but mounted further out on the Zodiac to protect its more elaborate and slightly longer tail-end embellishments.

40

41

42

43

44

45

46. The six-cylinder engine necessitated a considerably longer bonnet. The counter-balancing of the top can be seen here, and the paper-element type air cleaner over the carburettor denotes a late Mk2. The larger brake fluid reservoir, and the vacuum tank in the nearside indicate a disc-braked car.

47. The vacuum servo on the disc-braked cars fits between the battery and the front bulkhead.

48. At the other end of the car, a cavernous boot is a useful Mk2 feature, also complete with a counterbalanced top. The original spare wheel of this 1961 Zephyr makes an interesting comparison with today's low-profile tyres.

49. A central jacking point each side, and a sturdy jack with a simple circular motion made wheel changing easy.

50. & 51. The number plate was lowered to reveal the filler cap. On very early Mk2s the plate had to be held in the open position, an arrangement which however soon gave way to the over-centre spring device pictured here. The number plate illumination lamps are in the overriders – another neat touch.

52 & 53. The Low-Line Consul in estate car configuration. The rubber-covered roof slats, roof rail and strap eyes are all standard Farnham estate car features. The retention of the saloon's high back panel, and a side-hinged door made loading these estate cars not quite so convenient as the rather more purpose-built Australian versions.

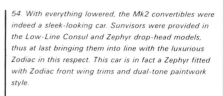

54.

55.

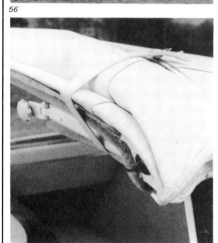

56.

57.

58.

59.

60.

61.

62.

54. With everything lowered, the Mk2 convertibles were indeed a sleek-looking car. Sunvisors were provided in the Low-Line Consul and Zephyr drop-head models, thus at last bringing them into line with the luxurious Zodiac in this respect. This car is in fact a Zephyr fitted with Zodiac front wing trims and dual-tone paintwork style.

55, 56 & 57. By simply pressing a switch the hood could be made to raise or lower automatically to or from the de-ville position.

58. The forward side rails and front portion folded neatly to be strapped in the de-ville position.

59. Fully closed, the convertible offered weatherproof motoring and all the usual saloon amenities.

60. The facia layout was as on the saloons, and this view shows well the steering column shroud covering the early type gearchange linkage which reappeared on the Low-Line cars. The steering wheel on this particularl Zephyr is in fact from an earlier car, and shows the elegant full circle horn-ring usually only found on the pre Low-Line cars.

61. The hood and side screen stowage resulted in a narrower rear seat than in the saloons. The front seat back is split, with each side capable of being tipped forward to allow quite easy access to the rear compartment via the wide, and heavy, doors.

62. Some boot space was required for the hood, and resulted in the convertibles being fitted with a non-counterbalanced boot lid with external hinges and a ratchet type supporting strut.

63

64

65

66

67

68

69

70

71

63. A handle was provided to lift the non-counterbalanced lid. The rear window is in safety glass, and the hood is in a heavy-duty PVC coated material.

64. Viewed head-on, the drop-head cars looked just as the saloon. The bonnet motif is a Ford accessory item.

65. Was there ever a more handsome British convertible than the Mk2 Ford? Many people insist there wasn't.

66. & 67. The Mk2 model was a popular choice amongst police forces. Here we see an early Zephyr belonging to a Continental Force, and a Low-Line Zephyr of the Victoria State Police in Australia.

68. Being able to carry large amounts of equipment such as temporary bollards, road cones etc., the Mk2 Zephyr estate car was a particularly useful road-traffic patrol car and was used extensively as such in Britain. The car pictured here was in service with the West Riding Police in Yorkshire during the 1960s.

69. The versatile Zephyr was an excellent competition car too, and here a "works" mechanic carries out adjustments on a Zephyr rally car fitted with a triple SU carburettor arrangement. This is the car which Gerry Burgess drove to second place in the over 2000cc GT category on the 1961 "Monte".

70. Jeff Uren on his way to winning outright the BRSCC Saloon Car Championship in 1959. Under the bonnet is a 168bhp Raymound Mays-tuned engine, and beneath the car can be seen the additional, lower anti-roll bar, and the shortened exhaust system which ran diagonally underneath to terminate ahead of the offside rear wheel.

71. Anne Hall raises the dust in East Africa as she gets in some practice for the 1961 East African Safari. This is the actual car which Anne used on the event in which she finished third overall to take the Ladies Cup and head the Zephyr's Team Prize-winning performance. The headlamp hoods are blacked to eliminate reflections, and a fine-mesh screen covers the grille ahead of the radiator to prevent mud, insects etc. from clogging the radiator itself.